Jack

Come 'ere till I tell you
Simple chats about God things

the columba press

First published in 1998 by
the columba press
55a Spruce Avenue, Stillorgan Industrial Park,
Blackrock, Co Dublin

Cover by Bill Bolger
Cover photograph: Marie McDonald
Origination by The Columba Press
Printed in Ireland by Colour Books Ltd, Dublin

ISBN 185607 236 3

Contents

Introduction

When I was attending a small rural national school many moons ago, there were two teachers on the staff. The principal was a first cousin of mine, and the assistant was my mother, who was an aunt of her boss. I myself became a teacher several years later. I taught all grades, from four-year-olds to eighteen-year-olds. I was ordained a priest at forty-one years of age, and, guess what, I went back into the classroom for the next fifteen years. This is my way of telling you that I am a teacher by training, and by instinct! Even when I did the Retreat and Mission circuit, around the country; when I took up an appointment in a parish; when I eventually moved to work with the elderly, ... in all of that work, I discovered, that I was still thinking like a teacher! (A teacher should never presume that the pupils know what he's talking about. The answers presented in the exams he sets should dispel that delusion!)

All of this became more evident, and, indeed, more useful, when I began writing, and recording cassettes. No matter what the medium, my approach has always been the same. With a subject like religion, I had never allowed it to become academic, like many of the other subjects on the school curriculum. My favourite method of presenting the core message of the gospels was to sit on one of the desks at the top of the room, and just share what I believed in, where I had come across the message, and why I believed it. I shared what I saw as the consequences of that in the lives of others, people I knew, and, indeed, people they knew. I shared with them, also, of course, the consequences I myself experienced. I then tried to lead them to 'give it a try'. 'I cannot tell you what this will do for you. I can only speak for myself. The only way you are ever going to find out what this will mean in your life is to try it yourself.'

I enjoy my work enormously, whether it be the spoken or the written word. The gospel is good news, and it is not intended as good advice. I have reason, by now, to believe that what I say, and what I write, is helpful to somebody, because I'm kept fairly busy! I tend to write exactly the way I talk, so the only big difference is whether you have your eyes open or not, (and you get someone else to do the reading!). I have named this book *Come 'Ere Till I Tell You*, so you imagine me sitting on one of the front desks, as you read!

From my own experience, I would hope this book serves a purpose, especially for our present hard-pressed catechists. It could also help in the preparation of homilies. Many of the stories in other books of mine are scattered throughout these chapters. I have deliberately chosen to include these stories, even at the risk of having over-used some of them. The alternative was to omit them, and I believe, by doing so, the material in this book would be enormously impoverished. I myself have used many of the same stories in my own teaching and preaching, and, I believe, they still prove effective. You can take it that most people are not good at remembering stories, and so the listeners may not be too sure just where they heard that one before! The correct story, placed within the teaching, can be a powerful vehicle for highlighting and reenforcing a message. I am hoping that what I now present may be inspirational for any reader of any age, who is open to reflection and prayer. Without this dimension in our lives, I don't think we can claim to be really living, and certainly not fully alive.

1 The snake in the grass

I want to begin by looking at human nature, and try to understand why we are the way we are, and why we do what we
do. I will speak of our human nature, as if it were 'out there',
apart from us, something we can hold away from ourselves,
and examine. In the following chapter I will look at how we
are managing our human nature, and how we might be able
to do a better job. Let me bring you back many years, to when
I was a child. I was one of a family of thirteen children, and
we were being reared during the war .... the Second World
War, I hasten to add! Anyhow, things were scarce and most
items were rationed. In other words, we were allowed a certain amount of bread, flour, butter, sugar, etc, for every member of the family. As most of us kids went off sugar during
one Lent or the next, and most stayed off it, my mother still
collected her rations of sugar, and we used have a whole lot
of home-made jam those days. Home-made bread was the
normal bread available those times, because the loaf, available in the shops, limited as it was, was a brown, sticky, half-
baked thing that weighed like a wet sod of turf. Anyhow, my
mother baking bread was a ritual to behold in our house.
Because of all the kids, there was plenty of flour and buttermilk needed, and the bigger the table on which to work, the
better. For me, as a kid, the most exciting part was when the
raisins were added. My mother was generous with these, unlike some neighbours, whom we believed, as kids, had just
put the dough in the oven, and, as an after-thought, a few
raisins were thrown in on top.

   Let us stop the operation for a moment, to reflect on how I

see this now, many years later. Life is a journey, and the further up the hill I climb, the more of the countryside I can see, in the distance. The mixture of flour, buttermilk, soda, salt, and raisins was called dough, and it had nothing to do with money! That was in the days when software meant cotton underwear, heavy metal was steel girders on a building site, and B.S.E. meant 'blame someone else'! If I take the dough, just before it goes into the oven, may I suggest that it represents our human nature, and the raisins represent the weaknesses that are part of what we are. From a health point of view, the dough should have a government health warning on it! There are aspects of our nature that can be quite destructive, like anger, jealousy, or deceit. We will follow through on this idea for another while. OK? My mother then took a rolling-pin, and rolled out the dough into a large thin layer. Then, with a tumbler, held upside down, and dipped in dry flour, she proceeded to cut out scones. I would suggest that each one of us could be represented by one of the scones. I hope you are not too offended by being compared to a scone! Anyhow, each scone has its own selection of the raisins, just as each of us has our own divide of human weaknesses. The raisins in one scone are obviously different raisins from those in the next one. In a family, one son can be a helpless alcoholic, or drug addict, while his brother still has his Confirmation pledge, and, who knows, he may even still have his First Communion money! From a very early age, one lad can show signs of being a real book-worm, while the other has never shown the slightest interest in learning, or schoolwork of any kind. Now, it is important to remember, that each has an equal divide of the raisins, that each has his own personal weaknesses, that none has escaped. One lad may be a drug addict, or he may be continually testing authority, and his brother may appear to be a real angel, when compared to him. However, if all the truth was known, the drug addict may have more good nature in his little finger than the other lad has in his whole body. One may be so good at keeping the good side out, and at hiding the shady side, that it might take a while to really get to know such a person, and to discover what sort of person he really is. I have often seen pupils in school, who seemed to be always in the wars. The truth could well be that, such a person is so open, and lacks a sneaky cunningness, and is always getting caught! I have always had a quiet admiration for such people.

It is a generally accepted fact that, if we gathered a group of people in a room, and if we could actually swop weaknesses with each other, that, before an hour is over, all would be demanding the return of their own personal weaknesses! We say that God fits the back for the burden, and we also say that it takes all kinds to make the world! The human race is like a huge mirror, that is taken off the wall, and shattered into many pieces, and a separate piece is entrusted to each individual. Each person reflects a different part of God's creation, even right down to a finger-print, which, in each case, is uniquely different, and can never be duplicated. If we could put all the pieces together, I believe that we would then reflect the face of God. How impossible it is for one piece of the mirror to imagine what the whole mirror might look like! It is important, however, to remember, that, as a piece of that mirror, I have an equal claim on the whole mirror, on the whole creation, to be on this planet, as much as any other person that has ever lived. That is the great tragedy, and the terrible injustice, when one part of the mirror becomes a tyrant, or a dictator, and assumes the right to destroy millions of the other parts.

In the early story of creation, we are told that, when God created something, he saw that it was good. And, of course, it was good, because, as Herb Barks would say, 'God don't make no junk'. What happened to that creation, to the dough, before someone added the raisins? We call this original sin. We all have heard the story of Adam and Eve, and their disobedience, in the Garden. Now, what we must remember about the Bible, and especially the earlier parts of it, is that it is made up of stories that were told around camp fires, for thousands and thousands of years, by a people who were always on the go, from one place to another. The word that is used to describe them is that they were a nomadic people, just as, to this day, there are nomads wandering through the desert lands of the Middle East. They were a people without roots, without a fixed abode, and, of course, they could neither read nor write. The stories were passed from generation to generation, and, of course, those stories lost nothing in the telling. If there was a car accident down at the corner, witnessed by five people, you can be sure that not all five will give an identical account of what happened. There is one thing about the stories in the early part of the Bible, and, that is, that each contains a truth, even if the description of what actually happened is not literally true. For example, could Noah have built an ark that held two of every animal in the world, at that time, and could he have taken enough food on board to feed both animals and people for such a long time? It is very unlikely. The truth, however, is that God preserved those whom he had chosen, and how that happened doesn't really matter. Let me put it another way. Suppose there is an accident down the road, in which John Murphy falls off his bicycle, and is killed. Now, the truth is that John Murphy is dead. To tell his wife that he was really lucky, because he was killed by falling off his bicycle, instead of being killed by a bus, is very little consolation to her! The fact is, her husband is dead, and that's the bottom line. Were there actually two people called Adam and Eve, and did they really eat an apple from a forbidden tree, and mess up all of God's plan? Again, I would answer that it doesn't really matter, because all the story is telling us is that God's people tried to put themselves above him, and outside of his plan and purpose for them, and, in that way, the plan was rejected by them. The story tells us that Adam and Eve had two sons, Cain and Abel, and that Cain killed Abel. Did Cain actually kill Abel? Once again, I say, that what happened was that, when people turned against God, they then turned against each other. That is the truth being conveyed by the story, and it would be wrong to take the story as literal truth. There was a film made quite recently about four people wrongly convicted, and imprisoned, for a pub bombing in England. Some people were annoyed with the director of the film, and accused him of not sticking exactly to what happened, and embellishing the story here and there. If I look at the film, however, without the need to be exactly correct in every detail, then, of course, it does tell the story of what happened, and I end up knowing the story, who were imprisoned, for how long, and what brought about their release.

God's people believed a lie, foolishly letting their pride and ambition get in the way, and, as a result, they came under new management. They came under the sway of the father of lies. We are told, in the story, that up to that time, everything was open, innocent, and there was no fear. When they got it wrong, they hid, because they were afraid. For the first time, fear is mentioned in the Bible. Then they were embarrassed, because they had no clothes, and as part of the hiding, and, literally, the cover-up, they used large leaves from the trees to cover their nakedness. Right from the start of the fall, there was a great need to hide what was considered shameful, and embarrassing. None of this bothered them up till then, and, from that moment onwards, it is part of being human to cover-up wrong-doing, and to pretend that all is well. In the story Adam blamed Eve, and Eve blamed the devil, and we're doing that since! To this day, it is very difficult for a person to be able to face up to things, and to admit 'I was wrong, what I did was very wrong.' In an ideal world, if the fall had not happened, and people were totally free to admit to being wrong, there would never be a war, and we wouldn't need our prisons.

With this messing-up of God's plan, people were now in a state of conflict. God had created people with a sense of right and wrong. You may well ask why God had permitted people to mess up his plan? God's most special gift to us is our free-will. If I were created in such a way that I just could not do wrong, if I were programmed, like a robot, so that I could only perform in a certain way, then there could not possibly be love. I can love you, only if I am free to make that decision, and there is no pressure on me, from any angle, to do so. If someone sent me a card for Christmas because he felt he had to, whether he really wanted to do so or not, there is not much to rejoice about in that. I cannot really do good, unless I am free to do evil, and with that freedom of choice, I still decide to do the good. It is absolutely vital, in God's plan, that we have free-will, and that nothing should spoil or harm that, in any way. Anyhow, people now found themselves in a state of conflict, because when they did wrong, there was a little voice inside which kept telling them what the right thing was. We call this conscience. The word conscience is made up of two words, con and science. Science comes from the Latin verb *scio*, which means 'I know'. In other words, conscience tells me something that I know rightly, even if I convince myself that I don't. When Adam and Eve sinned, they hid, because they knew they had done wrong. When I was a kid, I had a dog that looked very guilty, everytime he did something wrong! One look at him, and I knew he was after attacking the postman, or stealing food from the kitchen table. When I approached him, he would lie on his back, half-expecting to be smacked. When I patted him, he immediately sprang up, and jumped all over me. He knew he was forgiven!

And so, I think it is important for us to know, that, despite the raisins in the dough, when we do wrong, we know it, and all the excuses in the world won't succeed in quieting that little voice of conscience. In fact, I would go as far as to say, that, until I begin to really listen to that voice, I will never really be at peace. I am not talking about sin here, because I will speak later about how we are damaged as a result of original sin, and why we do many of the things we do. All I am saying, for now, is that one of the results of the fall is that, if I am honest,

I know rightly when I do wrong, and, as Lady Macbeth said, as she tried to wash away the guilt of murder, 'All the perfumes of Arabia will not sweeten this little hand.'

There is a story in the gospel that I find very consoling. Jesus talks about a farmer who sowed good wheat in his field. Later that night, an enemy came, and sowed weeds among the wheat. Some time later, the wheat began to appear above ground, and, yes, there were the weeds, as well. His servants came to him, and asked 'Was that not good wheat that you sowed? Where have the weeds come from?' The farmer told them that an enemy had done this. They asked if they might begin to pull up the weeds, and he said 'No, leave them alone. Let them grow, and, later on, at harvest time, I will take care of the weeds. If you try to get rid of the weeds now, you would only end up damaging the wheat, as well.' The story has a very simple, and a very important message. When God created us, we were good, and we still are good wheat. However, because of what happened, raisins have got into the dough, or weeds have got into the wheat. That is not of our doing, and if we, ourselves, tried to get rid of our human weaknesses, we would end up neglecting, and, eventually, damaging the goodness that is in us. Our human weaknesses are too much part of us, to be able to remove them. It would be easier for me to amputate one of my arms or legs, than to remove one of my human weaknesses. Even if I could succeed in removing one of my limbs, I would still have all my human weaknesses, because they are even more part of me than an arm, or a leg.

The three pollutants that entered our human nature are sin, sickness, and death. They were not part of what God created. An enemy did this. When I think of sin, I must always remember, first and foremost, that sin is something that happened to me. I am a victim of sin, I am a victim of something that was not of my doing. I will speak, later in this chapter, about the sins that I myself commit, but, for now, I need to say, once again, sin is, primarily, something that happened, that was totally outside of my control. I am damaged, because of it. I would compare it to having a hole in the ozone layer of my spirit, and that damage is something that I, myself, cannot repair. If God hadn't decided to come back into the equation, and to provide a solution that would take care of the weeds, I would be hopelessly lost. I will never understand personal sin in my life, until I understand that I am more sinned against than sinning. What's wrong with me? An enemy has done this. What am I to do about it? Just don't pretend there are no weeds there, and don't try to live as if you can run the show yourself, and be humble enough to let the creator deal with re-creating what has been damaged.

Let me tell you a story, that may help to explain our condition. A man went to a doctor with a very serious problem, that deeply troubled him. He told the doctor that every part of his body that he touched was really very sore, and he was quite worried about that. If he touched his nose, his chin, his elbow, his knee, all were really painful. The doctor gave him a thorough physical examination, and, when he was finished, the man asked him if he had discovered what was wrong. The doctor said that he had. 'What's wrong with you', said the doctor, 'is that your finger is broken.' Once the man knew that his finger was broken, and that was attended to, the other parts of his body were quite OK. That, basically, is what I am saying in this chapter. It is very important that I know why I am the way I am. If I can really accept that simple fact, then, hopefully, the rest of my life may not hurt as much as it has.

Programmes like Alcoholics Anonymous, for example, have helped to highlight the fact that there can be something within that is not capable of being controlled, or fixed, by myself. There can be a tendency towards behaviour that is insane, even if I fully rejected any suggestion that I myself might be insane. I can be quite sane, in many ways, and be guilty of insane behaviour. A compulsive gambler, or an alcoholic, who keeps doing the same thing, and keeps expecting a different result each time, is guilty of insane behaviour. I remember seeing a Charlie Browne cartoon one time, in which Lucy told Charlie that what was wrong with him was, that he didn't want to know what was wrong with him. Part of the problem with our damaged human condition, is that it can blind us to the truth of what that condition actually is. For example, an alcoholic is usually the very last person to see in himself what everyone else has been looking at, for years. Part of the disease is that it blinds us to the very fact that there is a disease.

Humus is the Latin word for clay, and we are human, because, traditionally, our bodies were formed of clay, and, certainly, after some time in the ground, our bodies return to that condition. *Humilitas* is the Latin for 'of the ground', and humility simply means that I accept that fact, and know that I cannot lift myself above my human condition, no more than a stone can become a flower, or a flower can become a dog. It's a question of accepting the nature that I have, warts and all. I am no better or no worse than the next person, as each of us tries to come to accept the raisins we have been given, and to do what we can with the strengths that are ours. As a poster I once saw, put it, 'If life gives you lemons, make lemonade.'

Let me summarise what I have said up till now. The wheat is good. You are a good person, just as the wheat is still good, and the dough is still good, despite the weeds and the raisins. What I am stressing is, that, unless I accept the presence of the weeds or the raisins, I will never succeed in understanding the human condition, and I could bring myself to the point of despair in trying to correct something that is outside of my control. I remember a man, who is an alcoholic, asking someone else where his alcoholism came from. He wanted to know if it was something he inherited, or was it something he himself developed. The other man, a recovering alcoholic of many years, and a much older man, turned on him sharply, and replied, 'The question is not really where you got it, but do you have it, and, if you do, what are prepared to do about

it.' The first part of the answer is the most important part ...
do I have it? When it comes to human weakness, the answer
must certainly be that I have it, and, if I am honest, my own
experience of life should convince me, beyond all doubt, that
that's the way I am.

2 Shady characters

In this chapter I want to look at how you and I have added to the problem, by the sins we ourselves commit. Again, to understand this properly, it is important to keep in mind that, through no fault of my own, I am born into a sinful state. I am not using that as an excuse for all my sins, or as a reason why I can do anything I feel like doing, and blame it on my damaged nature. If I am to be anywhere near being honest, at all, I should be ready to take responsibility for many of the things I do, knowing that it is usually my own selfishness, greed, or jealousy that has caused the harm. Eve's real problem was, not that she did wrong, but that she shrugged off her own responsibility in the matter, by saying, 'The devil made me do it.'

Firstly, let us look at the dark side of our nature, the part that is sometimes called the shadow. It's like the dark side of the moon, the part that we turn away from others, and will not permit to be seen. We all have our shadow, and, unfortunately, it is a part of us that we may not easily accept, that we do not like, and that we may even deny that it's there at all. An excellent book, around for a while now, is called 'Make friends with your shadow'. It asks us to accept the way things are, and not to be afraid to get to know that part of us that we don't like. Did you ever hear the comment 'She's really very nice, when you get to know her.' The socket over there in the wall has a positive and a negative. If it hadn't that, there would be no power. Everything has its opposite. If there was no light, there would be no darkness, there would be nothing with which we just judge light. If there was no such thing as sickness, we probably wouldn't have the word 'health', because we wouldn't need it. If I have come through a war, I will appreciate peace all the more, just as if I was reared in poverty, I will strive to get a good job, and to better myself. I think, just as the shadow in me can cause me to project the bright side even more, the bright side should not deny the shadow, pretend it does not exist, and do nothing about it. In a subsequent chapter, I will speak about Jesus coming, and how he declared very definitely, that he was on the side of the shadow, that he came to reclaim those things in us that we reject, and deny. He showed this most strongly by hanging around with the outcasts, the unwanted, and the rejects of society. He showed strongly where his preference lay.

Anyhow, back to us. Because of original sin, there is some kind of rebelliousness deep within us, that shows a stubborn determination to have its own way, and is not very ready to listen to common sense. It is like an addiction, or a compulsion, that can fight with great cunning for its own survival. All diets start next Monday, and there are a whole lot of people out there who are definitely going to stop smoking next Lent! Anything only face up to things now, as that part of me bargains for survival. I heard of a man who read so much about the dangers of smoking that, one day, he made a firm resolution, and gave up reading! St Paul gives us a good and a very honest description of what he experienced within himself, and it would be worth listening to most of it. '… I am full of human weakness, sold as a slave to sin. I cannot explain what is happening to me, because I do not do what I want, but, on the contrary, the very things I hate. I am not the one striving towards evil, but it is sin, living in me. I know that nothing good lives in me, I mean, in my flesh. I can want to do what is right, but I cannot do it. In fact, I do not do the good I want, but the evil I hate. Therefore, if I do what I do not want to do, I am not the one striving towards evil, but sin, which is in me. I discover, then, this reality: though I wish to do something good, the evil within me reasserts itself first. Even though my real self rejoices in the good, I notice within me another drive that challenges that good, and delivers me, like a slave, to the forces of sin that are within me.' I thought I should quote that at some length, because it is so honestly human from someone who was a very great man of God. Paul goes on, later in that passage, of course, to rejoice that Jesus had come to his rescue, when he himself experienced helplessness.

There is always a struggle or tension in life, as I experience myself pulled in one direction, and then in another. There is a tension between what I want to do, and what I ought to do. I go into a shop to buy something, and may end up with other items that I want, but don't really need. I can, of course, makes choices, but it is not always easy. I would argue that it is not really the tensions that cause the problem, but any attempt on my part to deny them, or pretend they are not there. There can be a whole lot of denial in myself, because the biggest lies I tell are the ones I tell myself. I will never really be honest with others, until I begin by being honest with myself. To do wrong is one thing, but to deny that wrong, and pretend it doesn't exist, only makes things worse. I am not, at all, talking about guilt trips, or flogging myself for what I do wrong. All I am saying is that it is necessary for my own maturity, and inner peace, to recognise the tendencies within me, and to try to understand why I do what I do. It is frightening when I come across someone who is trying to justify very destructive behaviour. In recent times, on our television screens, we have had leaders in the former Yugoslavia, in Northern Ireland, in Rwanda, etc, seeking to justify something that is dreadfully evil. There has never been a bomb planted, or a bullet fired, that did not begin in the human heart. The heart of man (and woman) can be a source of real evil, and, I believe we have within us the seeds of our own destruction. Like St Paul, we can all identify some force within us, that seems to drag us down, to hold us back, or to compel us into actions we would rather not do.

Let me introduce the word 'sin'. Sin is a lie, in some form, whether the action itself is deceitful, or it is based on something that is untrue. Let me be very specific about this, and do so through examples. Original sin happened when Adam and Eve fell for the lie they were told. I am not saying they were blameless, because they must have had some idea of being independent of God, or the temptation would not have been tempting. In other words, if a person found a wallet containing five thousand pounds, what is done with that will be decided by what is going on in the person's heart, and not by what is in the wallet. If the finder decides to hold on to the money, that action will have to be based on a lie, and, of course, on a lie that suits the finder. He can convince himself that someone else would have found it, and probably would have kept it, anyhow, so what's the difference when the person who lost the money was not going to get it back, anyhow. Someone with all that money in cash must surely have plenty of it, and this won't really be missed, and so, I convince myself that I need it more than the other. Immediately, you can be certain, that the mind will begin to put together whatever argument leads to the bottom line ... I put the wallet in my pocket. That is a sin, right there, because it is saying something that is not true, and that I know to be untrue. A married man is having an affair, and he brings home flowers to his wife, and is particularly nice to her, just to reassure her that she is the only woman in this world for him. That is a sin, because it is not true. Don't forget what I am saying: bringing home the flowers is also a sin, because it is a lie. His conversations, promises, and undying love being promised to the other woman is also a sin, because he is not a free agent, and is acting out a lie, and is assuming rights he does not have. Just watch the roundabout ways he goes about things, the deviousness, the plotting, and the intrigue, and watch how restless, and on his guard he becomes, and then try to tell me that he doesn't know that what he's doing is wrong! The liar has to have a good memory, because it is important to repeat the same lie, or I'm caught. One lie usually requires several others to back it up, and so begins the path that continues original sin in new and various forms. And then there is all the injustice that flows from sin ... the money that is stolen ... the marriage and home that is wrecked ... the life that is lost, and the families that are bereaved. Especially the destruction within my own spirit when I go against my own conscience, and try to live with the lies. It is not possible to live with lies, and have peace in my heart. I believe that I am punished more by my sins, than for them. That is why it has happened, on occasions, that, years after a murder was committed, someone called into the police station, and confessed to what he had done.

When I speak of sin here, I am not at all speaking from a church point of view; in other words, the church says this is a sin, therefore, it is. I am speaking here, as a human being, who is supplied with a conscience, and with a set of justice weighing-scales somewhere within my being, and when I try to act, while ignoring that fact, little red flags, red lights, and warning bells draw my attention to that. In other words, if we had never been given the Ten Commandments, it would have made little real difference, because, I believe they are written in our hearts. I know it is right to honour my parents, and that it is wrong to kill, steal, or tell lies. Any mother will tell you that, one look at a three or four-year-old child, and it is obvious, a mile away, that he has been up to something. I remember, some years ago, watching a nephew of mine, trying to turn on a television set, without his granny noticing it. I was fascinated, as he talked to her, told her he loved her, gave her a book to read, and, all the time he was backing towards the television set, with his hand behind his back, ready to push the button. This was before they got a television set, with, what he would call, a 'mote control'. Anyhow, he succeeded in turning on the telly, and, but for the fact that he couldn't manage to control the sound, with his back still to the set, he might have got away with it!

I remember, on another occasion, watching two young

people open up the boxes, and assemble the parts of a computer. Again, it was fascinating, as, with the occasional glance
at the instructions, and their instinct for such things, the
whole set-up began to take shape. That same afternoon, they
were already printing out some fancy drawings and works of
art. The whole secret of success lay in following the maker's
instructions, using every part that had been provided, and
connecting them up in the correct way. It is the same with us,
God's very intricate creation. If we follow the Maker's instructions, and not try to take short-cuts, because we couldn't
be bothered to do things correctly, then we don't break down,
and we work peacefully, and at ease with ourselves. Sin is a
disease, as in dis-ease, or a lack of ease. It is a rasping grating
sound, disturbs the soul's tranquillity, and makes it even
more difficult for me to enjoy my own company. And that is a
fact. I can become totally ill-at-ease in my own company, and
I will require the help of a walkman (or a brain by-pass, as
I've heard it called!) to drown out any attempts at the still
quiet voice of conscience to get my attention. Sin is selfishness, where I put myself before another, and meet my needs
at the expense of someone else. There is always a destructive
dimension to sin, because selfishness, and self-will run riot,
tends to trample down the needs and welfare of others. I was
speaking to a little girl recently, who was being prepared for
her First Confession, and she insisted on telling me her sins.
A sort of dry-run practice for the real thing, the following
Monday night, if you know what I mean. Anyhow, I had one
very strong reaction within myself, as I listened. Why, oh
why do we call such things 'sins'? Why not call them 'things I
did that were wrong', and introduce the word 'sin' when the
harmful, destructive behaviour begins. It would be a great
tragedy to lose a sense of sin, and there are times when I fear
that this is what is happening. Planted bombs, scattering
human limbs in all directions, are defended as necessary for
the furtherance of some cause. What an evil, evil, lie! Human
nature, unbridled, and conscience, unheeded, can produce

ugliness beyond compare. The ugliness, and the evil is bad enough, but to try to justify it, on the level of some noble or high ideal, makes the whole thing sickening and disgusting. The problem is that those who do such things, and those who suffer the results of such atrocities, are all part of who and what we are. If I am not part of the human solution, then, be sure, I am certainly part of the problem. There is no in-between, when I can stand back, and look on, like a spectator. A sin is a sin, and if God wanted a society where each could act independently of the others, he would have given us Ten Suggestions, and not Ten Commandments.

We are all sinners, because we have inherited a nature that is drawn towards the selfish, and the easy way out. In a later chapter I will share how I see what God has done to buy us back from all kinds of slavery. I will also have to look at what happens when I face up to truth in my life, and stop hiding behind excuses and falsehoods. In the meantime, I just wish to stress that we are all sinners. One time, a minister got very discouraged by the lack of interest and response among his people, so he decided to give up his ministry, and look for work from which he might get greater job satisfaction. He was surprised, and disappointed, to discover that work was very hard to come by, and he had to settle for a job in the local zoo. Before he took over his new job, however, he was asked to help out in an emergency that had arisen. The chimpanzee had died, and it was not possible to replace him at once, so, in the meantime, the zoo would lose the custom of the children who came especially just to watch the chimp. Anyhow, the minister was persuaded to put on a chimpanzee outfit, and enter the cage, where all he had to do was lie down in the sun, get up now and then, and jump around a few times, and then go in the back for a rest. To his amazement, whenever he jumped or rolled around, he drew great crowds, and he began to think that he was now getting more attention than he had when he was preaching for all those years! He actually began to like the job, and to get into the spirit of it. One day, feeling in high glee, he jumped up, caught the overhead bar, and began to swing to and fro. He was enjoying the cheers of the crowds so much, that he got carried away, and began to put more and more energy into the swinging. And then, just as he swung high into the air, didn't his hold on the bar slip, and he went flying over the partition into the cage beside him. This cage contained a lion, and, as the lion approached, our friend was terrified, and forgetting that he was supposed to be a chimp, he shouted 'Help! Help!', and the lion whispered, 'Shut up, you fool, or you'll ruin everything. I'm a minister, too!' No matter what the other people look like, no matter how smartly they dress, or how correctly they behave, they share one thing with you and with me. They are sinners, with a nature that is subject to the law of gravity, which can bring them down without any great effort on their part. When I say that I am a sinner, I don't mean to say that I commit sin all the time, but that, unless I am on my guard, and open to truth and honesty, I can look at the greatest blackguard, or the most hardened criminal, and say, with total honesty, 'But for the grace of God, which came through family, rearing, or environment, that could be me.' When I really believe that I am a sinner, I will stop in my tracks, and think, before I attempt to throw a stone at anyone. Someone said one time that, when you point a finger at others, you are pointing three at yourself.

If what I write helps you see sin for the destructive thing it is, and helps you identify that in your own life, then it will have achieved what I set out to do. I am deliberately not talking religion here, as much as plain common sense, and appealing to that streak of honesty and fairness, that's also part of who and what we are. Despite our damaged nature, and our inclination towards getting it wrong, I also happen to believe that people are, basically, very good, and make great efforts to do the good. We all need to be reminded, however, because we can all drift into habits and behaviour that, after a while, are accepted as normal. A sin is a sin, just, as the poet said that a rose called any other name, would smell as sweet. My conscience can get hoarse from not being listened to, and I can begin to skim the surface of life, without any great depth, or sincerity. I can become indifferent, I couldn't care less, and I just couldn't be bothered, and that is the worst state of all. The opposite to love is not hatred, but indifference, and when I reach that stage, I am spiritually dead, and can no longer have any life-giving qualities. When I fail to, at least, try to be honest, and to be authentic, I am mediating death to those around me, and I am more of a burden than a blessing to those who share life's journey with me.

Two men stood at the street corner in a country town, as a funeral came up the street. One man asked the other who had died, and was told that it was Pat McCarthy. 'Ah, is Pat dead?' asked the other, as the hearse passed by (I hope he was!) 'What did he die of?' asked the first man, to which his pal replied, 'I don't rightly know, but, as far as I can gather, I don't think it was anything very serious!' What I write is very serious, and it demands our most urgent attention. The more listening, reflecting, and pondering I can do on all of this the better. There then comes a time when the ending of discussion has arrived, and the time for making decisions has come. One of the ways of ensuring that I don't act on a particular issue is by discussing it long enough!

3 Recycling

So far I have been speaking about the human condition, as a result of original sin, and how we can make matters worse, by not facing up to accepting the way we are. We now turn our attention to how God came among us to re-create his original creation, and to make all things new. The big words for all of this are Incarnation, Redemption, and Salvation. He did that because he loves us, and he did it because, quite frankly, we could do nothing about it ourselves. Only the Creator could recreate, and restore things to the way they were.

There is a legend about God, the master composer of music and harmony, and the conductor of the orchestra of the universe. God wrote a master-piece, and he got an orchestra together to perform it. The wind and the breezes were entrusted with the wind instruments, and the trees, grasses, and reeds were given the strings. The sea and the thunder were to take care of the percussion, while the pan pipes, and the larger horns were given to the birds and the animals. There was just one part of the orchestra that was given a free hand, and that was people, whom, God hoped, would accept the responsibility given them, and would blend in with the harmony of the music. The music began, and the harmony was heavenly. The blending of sounds, and the interaction of the instruments, was a joy to hear. Then, one day, a horrible rasping grating sound resounded throughout the universe, and all of the instruments fell silent. There was a sense of silent shock and horror, as each section of the orchestra wondered where that had come from. Soon the secret was out. It was people, who, through some crazy act of defiance and pride, decided to act independently of the composer, the conductor, and the whole orchestra. 'What will the conductor do now?', whispered the breeze. 'Will he scrap the whole thing, and just forget about it?' 'He may decide to start all over again', said the trees, 'or he may write a different score'. 'One thing he cannot do', said the grasses, 'he cannot go on, as if nothing had happened, because we all heard that horrible discordant note, and it will surely echo down the ages, till the end of time.' And, guess what God did? He reached into all the sounds that had been, and picked out that discordant note, and, using that as a theme, he wrote the most beautiful melody around it, and turned what was ugly and upsetting into a thing of beauty, and a joy for ever. That, in summary, is what God did. He turned failure into success, defeat into victory. He based his whole new plan on the very fault that messed up the first one. God continued to write straight on crooked lines.

I draw three lines on a page, or on a blackboard. On the top line I write the word 'God', and further along the same line, I add a letter, and write 'good'. On the third line I write the word 'evil', and, again, further along the same line I add a letter, and write the word 'Devil'. On the middle line I write the word 'humus', which means clay, and the word 'humilitas', which means 'of the earth'. As I look at this, I must remind myself that there is no way that I, as represented by the middle line, can lift myself upwards, towards the good. I am subject to the law of gravity, and, by myself, I can only slip downwards. I need to be filled, as it were, with the helium gas of God's Spirit to be able to have any lift-off power, to rise up out of the quicksand of my own selfishness. That middle line, called *humus*, for us humans, can be very deceiving, because it is a fact that, by myself, I can do good. Of course, I can. However, it is a human good, and, like everything human, it is mortal, and will die; it just won't last. A very real part of being human is that I will die, and so will everything

that, by myself, I have achieved. Even, already, most of the
evil of a Hitler or a Stalin is almost cleared out of the atmosphere of this world, and, soon, please God, future generations will know about it only by reading their history books.
An alcoholic cannot stop drinking on his own. His efforts are
human, they will not last, and, therefore, you can be sure he
will go back to drink again. Unless he joins something like
Alcoholics Anonymous, which relies totally on help from a
Higher Power, he will not succeed. A tape recorder with batteries will play, but don't depend too much on it, because it
will not last, and is liable to let you down at the most awk-
ward moment. On the other hand, a tape recorder that is
plugged into a power socket, will continue to play again to-
morrow, and won't let you down. In simple English, I do not
have within myself what it takes to overcome the weaknesses
within myself. I must depend on a power greater than myself, on a power that is other than my own.

I am not good with things electronic, and it is only very recently that I have ventured into the area of the word-processor,
and the computer. I couldn't imagine myself ever getting so
confident, and so efficient, that, if a computer broke down, I
would take it on myself to fix it. No way! I would call in the
supplier, or the maker, and expect that such a person, who
put the thing together in the first place, will now be able to
take it apart, fix it, and put it back together again. A human
being is the most complex of God's creation, and when that
system breaks down, I will never attempt to fix it, but will call
in the Creator, who will surely be able to re-create his handi-
work. Much of this is simply common sense, because, if I'm
honest, I must admit that sometimes even the ordinary everyday events of life can be too much for me. God saw the situation right from the beginning. We say that God is love, and
that requires much reflection, to grasp what it means. Love is
the ability to meet and accept another where that person is at,
exactly as that person is. It also includes being willing to help
that person move from there, if, and when she/he is ready.

God could have loved me from a distance, but he decided not to do so. He decided to come to where I'm at, to meet me as I am. Like a doctor, God does make house calls! To be in a body is to be incarnate, and, when I die, and leave the body, I will become a discarnate. God decided to take on a human body, to take on our damaged human nature, and we say that he became incarnate, and the announcement of that fact is called the Incarnation, when the angel appeared to Mary, and asked her if she would be willing to provide the body, for that to happen. What that means is, perhaps, best explained by the following story. It was Christmas Eve, and a man was wondering why God chose to come on this earth as a helpless baby, when, to come in great power, like a six-million dollar man, would surely get more attention, and stir up greater interest. He was thinking about this, when he heard some noises out in his back garden. He looked out, and saw that four green geese had landed in the deep snow that had piled up there over the previous few days. Obviously, they had been flying, with many others, from the north pole down towards the equator, and one had become ill, and, as happens with green geese, a few others joined in, rather than abandon the sick member. The snow in the back garden was piled high, and was very soft, so the geese were sinking in it, and could not manage to move around. He was a kind hearted man, and he was willing to help, even if it meant gathering them into his garage, and phoning some group that could help with such things. He went out into the garden, and, as soon as he appeared, there was total panic among the geese. He opened the garage door, and tried to herd them into the garage, but the more he tried to help, the more the birds were terrified, and were injuring themselves, in their attempts to fly away. The man was really upset, because he genuinely wanted to help, and, for one crazy moment, he wished he were a goose, so he could speak their language, and tell them that he was only trying to help. It then dawned on him why Jesus came the way he did. This way, he could speak our language, and he could show us, and teach us, why he had come, and how he could help us.

You remember me speaking about the raisins in the dough, in the first chapter of this book? Well, what Jesus did, was take on all the raisins himself, all of our human weaknesses. One day he came along to the Jordan river, where sinners from all parts were gathering, so that John the Baptist might baptise them in the river, for the forgiveness of their sins. It was very normal for this to happen in those times. Anyhow, when John saw Jesus lining up with the others, he was shocked, because John was a prophet, and he knew that Jesus was someone very special, and totally free of sin. John objected, and protested that it is Jesus who should baptise him. Anyhow, Jesus persuaded him that this was necessary, and that John would understand later on why this had to happen. Jesus then went down into the river, and, at that very moment, he took on all of the weaknesses of humanity upon his shoulders. As St Paul would say later on 'He that was without sin, became sin for us.' And then an extraordinary thing happened. As Jesus came up out of the water, the heavens opened, and the Spirit of God was seen to descend upon him, and God the Father was heard to proclaim from the clouds, 'This is my beloved Son, in whom I am well pleased.' At the very moment Jesus took on the load of our brokenness and sin, he received an out-pouring of the power of God, that enabled him carry that burden, and overcome each weakness, one by one. Now, it is very important to understand the point I am going to make next: From that moment, Jesus did actually personally experience every human weakness there is. As St Paul said 'He was like us in all things, but sin. He was tempted as we are…' Because he had taken on all of the raisins himself, there is not a sin you could imagine that Jesus wasn't tempted to commit, but, as he said later, at his trial, 'Who can accuse me of sin?' He was accused of being a drunkard, a glutton; he was angry in the temple, and terrified in the garden. If there is a human weakness that you have, that Jesus did not personally experience, struggle with, and overcome, then you cannot be saved. With one struggle after another, Jesus would show that the power within was greater than the weakness he faced.

The three main pollutants, like the weeds among the wheat, that entered the human condition, were sin, sickness, and death. He took on the sin, paid the price, and earned the right to tell me that my sins are forgiven, if I ask him. We say that he is the Lamb of God who takes away the sin of the world. In a way, he became a scapegoat for us. In some tribes, there was a custom of people coming forward, at a ceremony, placing their hands on the head of a goat, and thus transferring their sins to the goat, which was then driven into the wilderness. In a TV documentary, some time ago, I watched people from somewhere in the Far East, as they gathered by the seashore, each carrying a little home-made boat, complete with sails. The idea was that, through some incantation, they transferred their sins into the boat, which was then placed in the water, so that it drifted out to sea. There is a deep-felt need within the human heart to know and feel forgiveness and reconciliation. In Jesus' time, a lamb was sacrificed for the forgiveness of sin, and John the Baptist, being a prophet, announced to his followers, as he pointed to Jesus, 'There's the Lamb of God … there's the one who takes away the sins of the world.' All of us have one human weakness in common, we will all die. And so, death was the final enemy that Jesus had to overcome. Barabbas, who represented us sinners, walked away, scot-free, and Jesus took his place. The cross that was on Calvary was one that had been prepared for Barabbas. Maximilian Kolbe was in a Nazi concentration camp, when a man was being taken out to be executed. This man had a wife and family, and Maximilian, a Franciscan priest, stepped forward and offered to take the man's place. His offer was accepted: he died, and only a few years ago we saw the pictures on our television screens of that same man, now very old, crying at the ceremonies in Rome when

Maximilian was declared a saint. That man had experienced real love, and he could never forget it. It would be easy enough for him to understand what Jesus did for us, when he took our place on Calvary.

A young lad, who was reared by the sea, developed a fascination for boats. One day he decided to get a piece of timber, and carve a small boat for himself, as a toy. He worked long and tediously on the task, and, eventually, the boat began to take shape. He worked with great love, and his mind worked through his fingers, as he shaped the boat of his dreams. When he was finished, he painted it his favourite colour, and put sails of brilliant white on it. Now, at last, his work was complete. However, it was a boat, and he knew that boats belong in water, so he brought it down to the seashore, and placed it on top of the water. It was a joy to behold, and he turned to call his friends to come see the beauty of it, as it danced on the water. When he turned back, he was shocked, because, having sails, it had already begun to move out into the water, and was now beyond his grasp. In desperation, he called it by name (he had given it a name), forgetting that, of course, it wasn't about to turn around and come back to him. The sails were like our free-will, and he could no longer control it, as it drifted further and further away from him, out into the deep. He stood motionless, with a pain in his heart, and tears in his eyes, as he watched it vanish from his sight. He slept very little that night, as his heart was heavy, and the thought of the boat was always on his mind. It was weeks later, and the thought of the boat was still fresh in his mind. He was down town, and looking in the shop windows. Suddenly, his heart missed a beat, and his mouth opened in amazement, as he looked in a window, and guess what, there was his boat among a display of toys. He was riveted to the spot, and, finally, he came out of the shock, dashed into the shop, and asked for the boat, his boat. The shopkeeper said he had bought it, and it was now his, and, if the boy wanted it, he would have to buy it, just like the other items in the shop window. The boy rushed home to his father, told him about the boat, and asked what he should do. The father asked him if he really wanted the boat, and he said he certainly did. His father told him that, if he wanted the boat, he would have to buy it, and when the boy asked him how much he should pay for it, he was told that, if he wanted it badly enough, he should be willing to give everything he had to buy it. The boy immediately gathered up every money box he had, emptied them all into one box, ran down to the shop, placed the whole lot, without counting it, on the counter, and asked for the boat. When he got it, he rubbed it, kissed it, polished it, and ran all the way home, to show it to his father. 'So,' said his father 'the boat is now yours?' 'Yes,' said the boy 'it's now mine, except now it's mine twice over, because I made it, and then I bought it back, and I gave everything I had to get it.' And that is what Jesus can say about you and about me. 'You are mine twice over, because I made you, and when you were lost, I found you, bought you back, and I gave everything I have to get you back.' In the following chapter I will speak in more detail about how this happened, and how I can best co-operate with that. You see, there is nothing automatic about God, and he is super-sensitive to my free-will, to my right to decide for or against what he has in mind for me. God won't send me anywhere when I die, rather will he eternalise the decisions I make now, and the directions in which I choose to travel now. He does not give me anything, … he offers me everything. It is totally up to me whether I accept that or not. He stands outside the main door of my life, with hat in hand, as it were, and he will not come in until I open the door, and ask him to enter. Some people reach skid row, as helpless alcoholics, before they cry out for help. Incarnation means that God comes to where you're at, even if that is skid row. It is not possible for a person to cry out to God, and not be heard.

Jesus is the farmer who has come to take care of the weeds among the wheat, and to harvest the wheat itself. We are the servants, and he told us that if we ourselves attempted this, we would end up destroying the wheat as well. As the Lamb of God, he made it possible for us to seek and receive forgiveness for our sins. He showed, on many occasions, that he had full authority over the demons, as he ordered them, and they obeyed. He healed the sick, calmed the storms, and raised the dead. As I've said already, the one raisin that each of the scones has in common, that we all share, is that we will all, one day, die. We are mortal. And so, the final enemy was death, and Jesus had to take on this one as well. When he went down into the river Jordan, and took all of our weaknesses upon him, he took an enormous risk, because if the Father had not released the power of the Spirit at that time, Jesus would not have come up out of that river. He was genuinely like us, where he had put his divinity to one side, rather than carry it in his back pocket for emergencies. His second great risk was when he bowed his head in death, trusting that the Father would be there for him, and see him through. Most of what Jesus told us had to do with the Father's love and care for us. It was very important, therefore, that he himself show that his Father can be trusted. Anyhow, he passed through death, and came out safely on the other end, and returned to spend forty days with his apostles, to convince them, beyond all doubt, that, yes, he was alive and well. It was vital that Jesus prove convincingly that death was not the end, and that the best was yet to follow. The final chapter of this book will discuss this whole question of death in greater detail. For now, however, I want to stress that this was one of the more serious weeds among the wheat, and certainly is something that brings us, sooner or later, smack bang up against just how powerless we are. Jesus wasn't brought back to life, as Lazarus was, who still had to die. Jesus passed through death, into a life in which death is non-existent. 'Dying you destroyed our death, rising you restored our life.' Because of what Jesus has done, there is nothing impossible for us any more. If we accept the offer he makes, and join in the victory he offers, then we are free, we are no longer slaves to the weaknesses within us, we are redeemed, we are saved.

4 As good as new

In this chapter I would like to share with you some thoughts on a personal encounter, and experience of Jesus, as my personal Saviour. The gospels are in between two phrases, ... at the beginning 'Come and see', and at the end 'Go and tell'. The shepherds at Bethlehem were told the message by angels, which is a fairly reliable authority, but immediately they said 'Let us go to Bethlehem, and see this thing for ourselves, which the Lord has made known to us.' It is a long journey from the head down to the heart, from knowing something to really believing it. Knowledge up in the head is academic knowledge, the kind of knowledge I might need to answer questions in an exam. Knowledge down in the heart is experiential knowledge, the kind of knowledge I would have about the Grand Canyon, if I visited it, and spent some time walking around there, studying it. I could talk about it, but you would need to see it yourself before you could understand what it looks like. Of experiential knowledge it could be said that, for those who don't understand, no words are possible, while, for those who do understand, no words are necessary. You needed to have a car serviced, and I recommended a friend of mine, because I tell you he does a good job, and he does not overcharge. If you decide to leave your car with him, you are acting on belief in what I told you. When you get your car back, you discover that the mechanic did a good job, and he had not overcharged you. The next time you need to have your car serviced, you go back to the same man, and, this time, you are acting on faith, because now you know, you have found out for yourself, you no longer need anyone to tell you. Faith is acting on what I come to experience for myself, after I had acted on some kind of belief, if you know what I mean! It involves eventually getting down into my heart, opening a door there, and inviting Jesus to come in, and take over. Some years ago, I used accompany pilgrimages to the Holy Land. We would visit Bethlehem, Nazareth, Calvary, and all the places associated with Jesus, when he walked on this earth. After the group returned to Dublin airport, my final message to them was 'Now you have been to the Holy Land, you have no need to return there. From here in, the Holy Land must be in your heart, because, unless Incarnation, God coming to live in a body, happens in you, there is little point in going out to Israel, to celebrate something that happened there a few thousand years ago. If Jesus came to take on human nature, and human weakness, he must be allowed take on yours, or it will all pass you by.' There is nothing automatic about Jesus. Simeon, in the temple, said that Jesus came for the fall as well as the resurrection of many. It all depends on us, whether we accept or reject him. The morning after arriving in Jerusalem, with the pilgrimage group, we always began on the Mount of the Ascension. After visiting there, we used walk down a pathway, towards the Garden of Gethsemane, at the foot of the hill. Half-way down the path, we would visit a little church, which is built in the shape of a tear. It was in this spot that Jesus cried, as he looked across the Kedron valley, at the city of Jerusalem. As he cried, he said 'Salvation was within your grasp, and you would not accept it. Now your enemies will surround you on every side, and your temple will be destroyed, and will be left with not one stone upon another.' It is very realistic to look across the same Kedron valley today, thousands of years later, and see soldiers walking or driving around, heavily armed, because they know that their enemies surround them on every side. As for the temple, it is a complete ruin, that can never be re-built. Somewhere in the ruins is the Holy of Holies, that most sacred spot in a temple, where no Jew would dare set foot, and so they cannot enter there now, for fear of standing on such sacred ground. Therefore, they cannot go in to begin building, and the temple can never be re-built. It is a touching reminder, many years later, that there is no peace outside of Jesus Christ. On the very night Jesus was born, it was announced that he came to bring peace on earth to those of good-will.

It is about coming to know Jesus, not just know about him. Knowing about him is in my head, knowing him is in my heart. A group of men chatted one night about good and bad memories. As a result, people were asked to test their memories by reciting something they had learned earlier in life. One young man opted to recite the psalm 'The Lord is my Shepherd'. He had excellent diction, and a gift for the dramatic, and when he was finished, there was thunderous applause, and he had to recite it a second and a third time. The next man opted to recite the very same psalm. He was elderly, and stooped, and it was difficult to hear him, as he began 'The Lord is my shepherd, there is nothing I shall want...' There was something about the way he recited it that caused everyone to remain silent when he finished, and, indeed, some even whispered a quiet prayer. The young man who was first to recite the psalm, stood up, and explained the different reception to the two recitals of the same psalm. 'It's obvious to me', he said, 'that I know the psalm, but that old man, he knows the shepherd.' And, that, dear reader, is at the very heart of what I hoping to share in this chapter.

Jesus is a very personal God. He asked his disciples 'Who do people say that I am?', and when they told him, he followed up with the crunch question, 'And you, who do you say that I am?' At another time, as he spoke his message, some of those listening found it hard to take, and they turned and walked away. Jesus let them go, because they were free agents. However, he turned to those who remained, and asked them, 'Will you also go away?' In other words, he is speaking to you personally. It is very important to remember that the gospel is not just something that happened thousands of years ago. It can be that, as far as you are concerned, if you don't get personally involved. If, however, I believe that the gospel is now, and I am every person in the gospel, then it must take on a whole new life and urgency for me. I have my own blindness, in the many things I don't see, or don't wish to see. I have my own leprosy, in some of the less pleasant and pleasing aspects of my behaviour. I have my own demons of pride, jealousy, lust, or aggression. Yes, indeed, as in the gospel, Jesus of Nazareth is passing by, each and every day. Jesus did not, and does not, go around healing anybody. He went around, and goes around, with the power to heal, and it's up to the person on the side of the road whether he wants to be healed or not. Anyone who stopped him, and asked him, was healed. He doesn't give me anything; rather he offers me everything. Jesus said that he won't have to judge us at all, because the word he spoke to us will judge us. He goes on to say that, if he had not come, we would have an excuse for our sins, but, now that he has come and spoken, we no longer have any excuse.

There are many miracles in the gospel. If we look at some of these, we will notice that there are a few conditions for a miracle. The first condition is very very important. Peter had fished all night, and had caught nothing. He had failed. A little woman in the crowd had been ill for eighteen years, and had spent every penny she had on doctors, but was no better. She experienced failure. The centurion did all he could for his servant, and Jairus did everything for his daughter, and their best efforts just weren't good enough. That's the first condition, that I am convinced beyond all doubt that I don't have what it takes, that whatever I have, or whatever I'm doing, is just not enough. The second condition for the miracle is knowing that Jesus can do for me what I cannot do for myself. 'But, at your word,' said Peter, 'I will let down the net.' 'If I can only touch the hem of his garment,' said the little woman in the crowd, 'I will be healed.' 'Say but the word,' said the centurion, 'and my servant will be healed.' Knowing that I cannot, and believing that he can, are the two conditions that produce miracles, and that is just as true today as it was when Jesus walked around the hills of Galilee.

Jesus was very definite that he never said anything unless the Father told him. So he told us the story about the son who got it all wrong, and then, when he came to his senses, he returned to his father, and was met with a hug. He told about two men praying in the temple, where one was boasting about how good he was, and how much better than the other guy he was, while the second man fell on his knees, admitted he was a sinner, and asked God to have mercy on him. That second man, said Jesus, was the good man in the eyes of God. He spoke about a shepherd, who would leave ninety-nine sheep, to go in search of one that was lost, and, when he found it, he carried it back on his shoulders, rejoicing that he had found it. He was forever reaching out to the broken, and the lost, assuring them that it was for such as they that he had come. He said that the healthy do not need a doctor, but those who are ill, and that he had come to find the lost sheep of the House of Israel. Jesus was always getting into trouble with the Pharisees, and others who were very insistent on proper behaviour. They condemned Jesus for being friendly with public sinners, and the kind of person with whom no self-respecting Jew would associate. For example, if I was told that Jesus was physically, visibly present in Dublin today, and I wanted to meet him, to make sure that I would meet him, I would go straight to the Iveagh or the Star of the Sea hostels, or to the Simon Community, because wherever there are broken or marginalised people, be sure you will find Jesus there. Any hope I have of coming into a personal relationship with Jesus is in exact proportion to the extent that I can be honest, and get in touch with, and acknowledge my own brokenness.

Christianity is not about external behaviour, about producing nicer people with better morals. I could be a pagan

and be a very nice person. It is not about prayer and fasting. I
could be a Muslim, and fast for a month at a time, and pray at
fixed intervals during the day, facing Mecca. No, Christianity
is about something that happens inside. It is about Jesus
being allowed take on my human nature, and my weaknesses.
St Paul says that when someone becomes a Christian, that
person becomes a brand new person inside, … a whole new
life has begun. Just as Jesus came up out of the Jordan river
with the burden of human weaknesses on his back, and the
power of God in his heart, so with the Christian, who still has
his quota of human weaknesses, but he also has the power of
God in his heart. 'Check up on yourselves', says St Paul. 'Are
you really Christian, or are you just pretending to be? Do you
experience the power of God within you?' When Paul himself became a Christian, he could say 'I live now, not I, but
Christ lives in me.' Take someone like Padre Pio, or St
Francis, for example. The presence of Jesus within was so
real, that they also had the wounds of Jesus on their bodies as
well. There is a very real experiential level to this. In other
words, if I have this power within, I will know, and so will
those around me. This is not mere pie-in-the-sky stuff; this is
for real. If Jesus is present, I will know it, and I won't ever
have to presume it. Mary and Joseph made that mistake one
time. They were returning from Jerusalem one time, and they
presumed that Jesus was somewhere in the crowd, but when
they got home, they discovered he wasn't there at all, and
they had to spend the following three days looking for him.
By the way, I heard one time of a kid in school, when asked
what Mary and Joseph did when Jesus was lost, and she answered, with total confidence, 'They went down to the temple, and said three Hail Marys to St Anthony!' Well, anyhow,
they found him. I remember, many years ago, there was a
preacher man on the back of a lorry, down in the market
square of my own home town, and he was thumping the
Bible, and talking about finding the Lord. There was a local
man, at that time, who was simple, and who attended any-

where a crowd gathered, whether he was invited, was interested, or not. Anyhow, as the preacher got warmed up to this
subject, our friend was in the front row, with his usual vacant
stare on his face, and the preacher, not knowing him, mistook
this to be some sort of spiritual rapture. He turned to our
friend, and, with a dramatic gesture of his arms, he drew attention to him, as he asked, 'And you, my dear man, have
you found the Lord?', to which our hero replied 'Naw, did
you "loss" him?' It is never a question of me looking for the
Lord, as if he were the one always getting lost. I am the one he
is seeking, and he will come to me at any time, in any place,
and under each and every circumstance.

Jesus said that he would stay with us always, that he
would never abandon us. He said he would not leave us or-
phans, and then he offered us his father and his mother. He
told us, however, that it would not work unless we became
like children. One of the endearing qualities of children is
their capacity to trust, and to accept love. I remember, on his
birthday, some years ago, a nephew of mine just accidentally
mentioned that fact, in a phone call to me! I laughed, and was
sure that everybody on the road knew it was his birthday.
When he gets to my age, if he receives something for his
birthday, his concern will be to find out when the other person's birthday is, to return the compliment, because, with us
adults, there are no free lunches. We do not have the simplicity
and the humility of the child, who is delighted with free gifts,
and the more the merrier. A father and mother, with their six-
year old boy, went to the supermarket to do the weekly shopping. They were pushing a shopping trolley, as they loaded
on their groceries. Eventually, they arrived at the check-out,
and the father began putting the items on the conveyor belt
for the girl to check them. Just then she turned to him, and
said 'There's no charge today, everything is free.' The father
smiles, telling her she is really funny, as he continues to take
the items out of the trolley. Once again, the girl says that the
goods are free, and, by now, the father, who is nobody's fool,

is glancing around, convinced that this has got to be one of those candid camera set-ups. He glances at the girl, to ensure she has a name-tag. Maybe she has had a row with her boss, and this is how she is showing her defiance. By now, the father is beginning to think that enough is enough, and all he wants to do is pay for the groceries, and get out of here. And where, I ask you, is Junior? He heard the magic word 'free', and he has just grabbed another trolley, and is flying around the supermarket, filling it with all the things he loves! That, says Jesus, is the heart of a child, who is totally convinced that, as I cannot earn it, I have to depend totally on getting everything for free

St Augustine said 'You have made us for yourself, O Lord, and our hearts will never be at rest, until they rest in you.' There is something within the human heart that longs for what God is offering, because we know that God is offering something that we need. The gospel tells us that Jesus came to his own people, but they would not accept him. But to those who did accept him, he gave the right to become children of God. All they need do is accept him, and let him do what he came to do. Jesus has done all he can, and, now, it is up to us whether we accept that, or not. St Paul says that the formula for salvation is his blood and our faith. It is what he has done, and whether I believe that or not. Someone can come up with a cure for cancer, but nothing happens until I take that medicine. Despite all he has done, I can still choose to go it alone, and live as if Jesus hadn't come at all. At Cana of Galillee, Mary told the waiters at the wedding to do whatever Jesus told them, and everything would be alright. In his day, there were many people who died of leprosy, or died as blind people, simply because they never asked him, and he just passed on down the road. From that first Christmas night, there have been many doors and many hearts closed against him. The average person going down the road believes in God, but may not be very convinced that they need him just now. Jesus offers me peace, but I'm totally free to live

in misery, and die of ulcers, if I want to. He didn't want Judas
to go out to hang himself, but he wouldn't stop him, because,
in no way will Jesus bully us, or brow-beat us into listening to
him, or accepting him.

There is one major problem with accepting the gospel, and
Jesus spoke about that. He thanked his Father for giving a
message that is so simple, that intellectuals, or those using
the wisdom of the world, will never be able to understand. In
other words, it makes no sense at all up in the head. Indeed,
Simeon, in the temple, said that Jesus would be a sign of contradiction, because everything he does and says is so different from the so-called wisdom of this world. Unless I come
down-stairs into my heart, I will not meet Jesus. Jesus did
none of the great things the world proclaims, like leading an
army, ruling a nation, or accumulating wealth, yet he is spoken of today all around the world, centuries after he appeared on this earth. Philosophers, theologians, and other
people of wisdom, over the centuries, have discussed every
word he said, and million of books have been written about
him. However, and I think this is funny, if I had the simplicity
and humility of a child, I would learn more about Jesus, by
turning to him, myself, than I would from all the books in the
world. Kierkegaard, the philosopher, in speaking to Hegel, another philosopher, one time, said, 'Aren't we philosophers
extraordinary geniuses. We can take the simplest concept,
and by the time we have put it in words, you can be sure no
one will know what we are talking about. Last week, I was in
Copenhagen, and I asked another philosopher for directions
to a street not very far away, and he gave me a map of
Europe!' We can do the same with the message of Jesus. We
can discuss it till the cows come home, and forget that Jesus
wants decisions, not discussions. 'You are either for me or
against me,' he said. When some of his followers walked
away, because they considered what he was saying as too difficult for them to accept, he let them go. Instead, he turned to
those who remained, and challenged them about where they

stood, because their not leaving may not have been a definite decision to stay. Someone said that there are three groups of people in any society. There is a small group who cause things to happen, there's a larger group who watch things happening, and there's the vast majority who haven't a clue what's happening! Jesus will always challenge us to make up our mind, to decide for or against, because there's no in-between, as far as he is concerned.

In several of the remaining chapters in this book, I will be returning many times to the concept of Christian commitment, and to the various ways in which it can be approached. The plain fact is, that, we have nothing, and are nothing, outside of Jesus Christ. If he hadn't come to the rescue, the gates of heaven would be eternally closed against us. When he went down into the river Jordan, the heavens were opened. When he bowed his head in death, the veil of the temple was torn in two, and for the first time, any one of us can enter into the presence of God. Jesus said that he is the way, and that no one can come to the Father except through him. He is now our Moses, leading us through the desert of life into the Promised Land.

5 Free at last

Remember what I said about original sin involving believing a lie, and, therefore, coming under new management? How Adam and Eve hid, and that, in some ways, we are still hiding, as we find it particularly difficult to own up to truth. The influence of the kingdom of darkness was very tangible and real, right from that moment on. Jesus came to answer the lie. He spoke in a very direct and straightforward way. He said that Satan was a liar, and the father of lies. He asked us to stop hiding, to come out into the light, and let his Spirit of truth lead us, and we would be free. He invited us to come back to the Garden, and he assured us that there was a great big welcome waiting for us there, even if we did get pig's food all over our faces. When I was a child, I learned in my catechism that God is immutable. I didn't understand what that meant, at the time, despite every effort to explain. Anyhow, now that I can look up a dictionary, I know that it means that God does not change, that he is the same yesterday, today, and always. God is creator, and he always will be. Will he destroy this planet? No, he won't, we'll do that ourselves … we're already working on the seas, the rain forests, and the ozone layer. God is love. Could God ever end up not loving you? No way. But, suppose someone ended up in hell, does God still love that person? God's love hasn't changed at all, even if, by deliberate choice, someone has put himself outside of that love. It's like a light shining on me here, as I write. If I went out the door, and closed the door behind me, the light is still shining, and has not changed in any way. It is

I that have cut myself off from the light. I remember seeing a poster one time of a cat lying down, looking up at me, and written on the poster were the words 'Does God seem far away?' Down at the bottom of the poster, in small print, were the words 'Guess who moved?'

Jesus lived on this earth for thirty-three years, three of which were spent in public ministry, when he passed on to us what the Father told him to tell us. Now, supposing he had been given three minutes to deliver his message, rather than three years, and there was a stop-watch on him, to check the time exactly, and after that, he had to leave, to return to his Father. What do you think he would have said in those three minutes? I really don't know, but I would like to think that he might have told us the story of the Prodigal Son, because that, I believe, is the gospel in miniature. It is the story of someone who used his free-will to do his own thing, to do things, and to live his life, as he chose. He wandered far from base, and things went from bad to worse for him. Eventually, he hit bottom, when he found himself eating the food left behind by pigs. As a Jew, he grew up believing that pigs were unclean, and must be avoided at all costs. To be taking care of pigs was bad enough, but the idea of a Jew actually eating the food that was given to the pigs was really rock-bottom. The story tells us that 'he came to his senses', in other words his eyes, ears, and other senses woke up to the plight he was in, and the horror of it hit him, with full force. He decided there was no future for him down that road, so he made a decision. He decided to face up to the truth of what had happened, and to get out of there, and return to what he had left behind. His guilt and disgust was very real, and he doubted that he could regain what he had thrown away. He came home to face the music, and to take his medicine, believing that he had earned rejection, and condemnation. Imagine his surprise and delight, when he was met with a hug, and with a sincere and warm welcome, without a word of condemnation. It must have taken some time for this to sink in, but, no doubt, he came to accept that the welcome was sincere, and he had actually come home to even more than he had thrown away. It is a very touching, and human story, and Jesus intended it to leave us in no doubt about the kind of God we are dealing with.

Original sin was about falling for a lie, and coming under the influence of Satan, the father of lies. Salvation is about being led by the Spirit of truth, out of that kingdom of lies, and being led into truth, and, as Jesus said, the truth will set me free. Like the Prodigal Son, I, too, can come to my senses, and be willing to look at myself honestly, and to face up to what I see there, There was a man who went to work every morning, with his lunch-box under his arm. Every day, at lunch-time, in the canteen, he went through the same routine. He opened the box, took out a sandwich, unwrapped it, separated the two slices of bread, and moaned to himself, 'Oh, no, not cheese again!' This went on day after day, until his workmates got annoyed with him. One of them asked him why he never asked his wife to put something else in the sandwiches. 'What wife?' replied the man, 'I'm not married.' 'And who, then, makes the sandwiches?' asked his pal, to which he replied 'I do.' Coming to my senses is about looking at my life, and seeing who is making it the way it is. It is about taking responsibility for my actions, and when I am wrong, being willing to admit it. There is a vast difference between saying 'I did wrong', and 'I was wrong.' I could admit that I did wrong, and then go on to blame you, the government, or the weather for causing me to do it. Admitting that I was wrong, is to take personal responsibility for my actions, and to ensure that the buck stops with me.

I remember a man coming to me, some years ago, and he was drunk. He wanted me to pray with him, and when I asked him what he wanted me to pray for, he said 'For will-power, Father.' I smiled, and said that, of course, I would say a prayer with him, but first I asked him to go away, and think about what he was doing with his time and money, and the following day, if he had the will, he should come back to me, and, together, we would ask for the power! If I have the will, God will give me the power to do anything. Guilt is not from God, and God is not at all into the business of laying guilt trips on anyone. Jesus was forever challenging people to look into their hearts, and to examine their behaviour. He interrupted the woman at the well, who was debating whether it was better to worship God in one place, in preference to another. He asked her to go call her husband, knowing that she had been married many times, and the man with whom she now lived was not her husband. In other words, stop the waffling, and don't try to gloss over the truth. He was not condemning her, but I feel he was trying to free her from a burden he saw that she was carrying, and was doing everything except face up to the truth as it was. Don't forget, truth and freedom go hand in hand, and it is for the freedom that he wants me to face up to the truth.

There are three different types of courage, animal courage, human courage, and moral courage. Animal courage is pure native instinct. A mother will dash into a burning building to rescue a child, without any thought about her own safety. A rat will attack, if cornered. There is no thought going into the process, it is just pure instinct, and we all possess this, to a greater or lesser degree. Next is human courage, the type that is needed to defuse a bomb, or talk an armed man into surrendering. This is not so common, and not everybody possesses it. Lastly, there is moral courage, the highest, and rarest of all. This enables me stand up for what I know is right, and condemn what I know to be wrong, irrespective of what others think. I am not speaking of the brutal honesty that some people glory in, where a point of view is expressed, irrespective of who gets hurt in the process. The ideal of proper communication is to strive to combine honesty with kindness. I could visit someone in hospital today, who asks me how I think she looks, and I could tell her that I think she looks awful, and that she'll probably die to-night! I could be totally honest in saying that, but it would not be the kindest thing to say. And again, if I were in a position of authority and responsibility, I could be so kind to others that I turn a blind eye to unbecoming behaviour, and unacceptable practices. In doing so, I may be kind, but certainly not honest.

When it comes to standing before God, the only requirement is that I be honest, no matter how broken I am, or how far away I have wandered. A sheep that is lost is inconsolable, because sheep have such an instinct for the flock. This was the image Jesus chose to emphasise how my heart can be, and how alienated I can feel when I have wandered from the truth. I can even be totally alienated from myself, as I flog myself with guilt, and self-accusation. I am convinced that the Lord longs to generate reconciliation within my heart. I am every person in the gospel. I am the Prodigal Son, and his self-righteous brother; I am the Pharisee and the publican; I am Martha and I am Mary. How the Lord would love if the self-righteous brother would hug the Prodigal Son, or the Pharisee would go to the back of the temple to embrace the publican. Reconciliation is about embracing brokenness, either in myself, or in those around me. It is about compassion and acceptance, that does not sit in judgement. It is this kind of love, and this alone, that will enable the ghosts of hurts and sin come forth to be dealt with. The Inner Child within each of us is very sensitive, and is terrified of scorn and rejection. That Inner Child wouldn't hurt a fly, and Jesus asks us to let such a child come to him, because the kingdom of heaven belongs to such as these. A mother was planning a night out, and was really looking forward to it. She went to a lot of trouble, and even made herself a beautiful dress for the occasion. Her little daughter, who was very demanding, and liked getting her own way, did not like the idea of mammy going anywhere without bringing her. She found the dress lying on the bed, and immediately she got a scissors, and cut lumps out of it. It was several hours later when the mother discovered what her daughter had done. She was shattered, and she just threw herself on the bed, sobbing her heart out. The little girl heard her, and entered the room, and became deeply ashamed of what she had done. She approached the mother, who just turned her back on her, and ignored her. No matter how she tried, the mother continued to cut her off. Eventually, the little girl grabbed the mother's arm, and began begging her 'Mammy, mammy, please take me back, please take me back.' The mother knew that the cry came from her little heart, so she turned and embraced her, as they cried together. The girl, somehow, knew that what she had done had put her outside the pale, and she desperately needed to be let back in again. She knew there was no life for her outside of her mother's love and acceptance. It is the same with ourselves and God. He is longing for us to ask to be taken back again, and his arms are always stretched out in a gesture of welcome.

Faith is a response to love, and Jesus has died to show us how much he loves. 'God loved the world so much', Jesus told Nicodemus, 'that he sent his only son, so that they who believe in him might have eternal life.' I remember seeing a poster one time which said 'I asked my God how much he loved me, and he stretched out both arms fully, and said "This much", and then he died.' Greater love than this no man has, that a man should lay down his life for his friends. 'You are my friends...', said Jesus. He has called you friend, as he invites you into a deeper personal relationship with him. The betrayal of Judas was made all the more ugly by being paraded as friendship, when Judas walked up to him, and kissed him. Even then, Jesus called him friend, and Judas would have been warmly embraced if he were prepared to face up to what was going on in his life. Judas betrayed Jesus, and then ran away, and put himself outside any hope of Jesus being there for him. There is a theory in Orthodox spirituality about the end of time. The throngs are making their way into heaven, and Jesus is seen to be standing there, looking off into the distance. Someone asked him what he was doing, and he said 'I am waiting for Judas'. Jesus showed through everything he said and did, that he had a special place in his heart for sinners, who were ready to come home to the truth, to where they belonged. 'I did not come to condemn the world, but to save it', he said. Sinners were drawn to him, as to a magnet, and he himself was condemned and crucified for nothing more than that he hung around with sinners, and, as the gospel says, 'even eating with them'. He befriended and defended those who were rejected and condemned by the religious leaders of his day. They discovered that they were accepted by him, and were safe in his presence.

How often is the word freedom used in connection with Jesus! Before he was born the prophets spoke of a Messiah coming to set them free, to free them from slavery, to free them from the oppression of their enemies. John the Baptist's father Zachary said that the Messiah would free us from fear, and from the hands of our foes. We are told in Scripture that if Jesus sets you free, you will, indeed, be free. How many thousands of members of Alcoholics Anonymous throughout the world can vouch for the way the Lord has set them free from a slavery over which they had no control. Jesus came to set us free, because, in many ways we can be prisoners ... prisoners of fear, guilt, depression, or of self-will run riot. In the Mass we say 'Lord, by your cross and resurrection you have set us free, you are the saviour of the world.' Imagine the following story. This man is in prison, awaiting execution. He has led a violent life, and he is about to meet a violent end. One morning he hears a loud commotion up in the court-yard overhead, and he is convinced they are coming to get him. He can hear timber being prepared for a cross, and he knows that is the kind of death that awaits him. Eventually the long-dreaded sound is heard approaching. It is the march of soldiers coming to bring him out. His name is Barabbas, and this is the end of the road for him. The door of his cell is opened, and one of the soldiers beckons him to come on out. In fact, the soldier is actually telling him to go home! There's no way he's going to fall for that old shoot-in-back-when-I-tried-to-es-cape-trick. He refuses to budge, even when the soldiers tell him plainly that he is free, and all charges have been dropped. Eventually, the soldiers grab a hold of him, and throw him out. He lurks in the shadows, sure there is some catch in this. The cheers and shouts of the crowd have faded away as they apparently went out the country. It is some hours later, and he is still skulking in the shadows, when he spots a former bandit friend of his passing by. He catches his attention, and when he comes over to him, he asks what has been happening all morning. His friend seemed amazed that Barabbas was unaware of what has just happened. He brought him outside the town, and pointed to three crosses on a hill. 'Do you see that cross in the centre? Well, that was the cross they had prepared for you, but that man took your place. Now, you really are free, and, if you take my advice, you'll get going when the going is good, and make use of the freedom that has been earned for you.'

Which reminds me of an incident from my early child-hood in the country. This man used come around buying hens. He would buy a hen, tie her legs, and toss her in the back of his cart. One day, he decided to give us local yokels a lesson in hen psychology, so he reached in with a scissors and snipped the twine tying the legs of one of the hens. I was amazed when I saw that she didn't move, or make any attempt to fly away. Actually, he knew the hen wouldn't move, because, understanding hens more than I did, he knew they were stupid, and a hen would never realise she was free if all the hens around her were still tied up. If he had snipped the twine on the legs of all the hens, they would all have flown away. It can be the same with me. In the midst of people burdened with worry, guilt, anxiety, and alienation, I can completely forget that I'm as free as I want to be, I am as free as I myself will allow myself to be. God gives me nothing, while offering me everything, and it's totally up to me whether I accept it or not.

In the next chapter, I will deal, in some detail, with reconciliation with God, myself, and others; about repentance, conversion, and, in general, how I can rid my life of the wreckage
of the past. In a later chapter I will have much to say about
hope, about being highly optimistic in the midst of our brokenness, and about how God himself, in Jesus, is walking
with us every step of the way. When Jesus asks me 'Who do
you say that I am?', I want to be able to tell him that, yes, he is
my personal saviour, and my heart is one place where I really
want Incarnation to take place. Like Mohammed and the
mountain, I couldn't get to God by himself, so he has to come
to me. With all my heart, I want to welcome him into the brokenness, the sin, and the hurts, and let him get on with salvation there. I want to believe that he means every word he says
when he tells me that it is for people like me that he has come.
Healthy people, he said, do not need a doctor , but those who
are ill. I have come to seek and to save those who are lost.

I join the Prodigal Son, and the publican, and I confess that
I am a sinner, and that I have sinned against heaven, and
against others, and that I certainly need a saviour. O God, be
merciful to me, a sinner. There was a man on another cross
beside Jesus on Calvary, who may never have said a prayer in
his life. He asked for help, and was offered heaven right
there. It is totally free, and I would be totally free, if I accepted
the offer.

6 Telling it like it is

I am hoping that the material in these chapters will appeal to Christians of all denominations and ages. At this point, however, I wish to speak about sin within the Roman Catholic Church. I will try to do so with love, but with honesty. In the next chapter I will explain the sad results that sometimes results from religion, when the emphasis is on the law, and strict observance of law. That emphasis has, unfortunately, been part of the approach with the Catholic Church over the years. In general, I have to admit that the church has not been good in its dealing with sins and sinners. In many ways, it has been seen to fail in the very area for which it exists. Jesus died to bring people over a bridge from a love of law, into a law of love, and, I'm afraid, that, by the time I came along, the church had gone back over the bridge again into a love of law. I don't wish to dwell on such obscenities as the Inquisition, and all the many ugly and unChrist-like ways the church has dealt with those who fell foul of her rules and regulations. Nothing, but nothing can defend all of that, and, I hope, it remains condemned for the evil that it was. Apart from such extremes, however, I still see many signs of other ways in which the church has been less than compassionate towards the sinner, down the years. Many of those have been during my own life-time, and some persist to this day. Now, it is not my intention to justify wrong-doing, or to defend behaviour that is wrong in its very essence. I speak more about the sinner here, than the sin. As a Christian, I must always be compassionate and forgiving, and I must remember that all judgement belongs to God. In fairness to the church, I must

,ut that it is always effected by the norms that prevail
y particular time in history. For example, to switch from
church, for a moment, let me make a comment on my
vn schooldays. I myself witnessed and received many a se-
vere physical attack from teachers who were entrusted with
my education and welfare. However, if I had brought that
fact to my parents for redress, I risked more physical punishment from them, for giving the teacher trouble in school! It
was a no-win situation, because that was a reflection of the
thinking and approach of the times. Children were to be seen,
and not heard, while parents and teachers were always right.
Naturally, the church, which was but an extension of home
and school, reflected the same approach. The rules, the laws,
the customs, the traditions, … all were above and before the
individual, and that's just the way it was. I look back, with
the benefit of hindsight, and I see things that still make me
angry, and still puzzle me. However, if I am honest, I must
admit that, many years from now, people will look back at
this time, and speak of things that were very wrong, but are
acceptable now. I do not know what those things will be, but I
could hazard a few guesses that they may include the exclusion of women priests, the absolute ban on married clergy,
the Sunday church attendance being of obligation, under
pain of sin, and many other things that, I imagine, may not
appear to be as important, when viewed many years from
now. In other words, if I leave the gospel out of the formula
(which would be disastrous), the church can easily become a
product of its time.

I cannot, and dare not, leave the gospel out, because, without that, there is not, and should not be a church in the first
place. The only reason for the church's existence is to pro-
mote the message of Jesus, and to point to him as saviour and
Lord. I really believe that, it is when the church lost sight of
its very reason for existence, that it became dogmatic, and
dictatorial in its dealing with people. I refer to the church as
'it', even though normally referred to as 'her'. I believe the

'her' comes from the concept of church as mother, and I do not use the expression now, while I speak of ways in which the church has displayed more of the characteristics of dictator than mother. I do not relish saying this, but I have to be honest, and so, I do not apologise. In the following chapter, when I share how I believe that religion usurped the place of Spirituality, it will be easier to see how the emphasis slipped, and why we went the way we did. The love and compassion of God was poured out on this earth on Calvary, and the blood of God soaked into the very earth. There is no longer room for self-righteous condemnation, and arrogant anathemas to be poured out on God's people. The fire and brimstone age came to an end when Jesus came among us, and, even the stones we would throw at those we condemn must be cast away, as we stand before God with open hands, ourselves in need of his salvation. Christianity is about attracting, not promoting. In the land of Israel to this day, the shepherd walks in front, and the sheep follow, rather than being driven from behind. It is what I am is my message, not what I say. If I enter your home, and tell you I have measles, while, actually, I have chicken-pox, which are you likely to catch?!

'Confession', as it came to be called, has had a bad press down the years. Even the very name reveals the wrong emphasis, where the stress is on what I do, rather than what the Lord does, when I come to him. Among the many current attempts to make it relevant to today's world, the title has now been changed to Sacrament of Reconciliation, because reconciliation is what God does. We are the ones who became estranged from God, and Jesus came to invite us back to the Garden, where we could be reconciled with a welcoming hug from the Father. Once the emphasis moved from God to us, it continued in that direction, until we had highjacked it totally, and God had very little say in it anymore. Our sins were what mattered, and we had pages and pages of questions, by way of examen of conscience, that we went through. Then we lined up our sins in some sort of order, and we then went into details about number and species. We had a whole lot of prayers to say before approaching the sacrament; we then were liable to face further cross-examination, not to say, a possible lecture, or scolding, which was followed by a penance, and then another few pages of prayers after we came out of the Confession box. My experience of Confession was far removed from what would have happened had I met Jesus on the roads of Galilee, where sinners flocked to him, to receive his compassion, love, and acceptance. In fact, his condemnation was reserved for those who were so perfect in their own eyes, that they considered themselves as not needing what he so generously offered. They sought every means within their power to contradict and oppose him, and to condemn him for the special place he reserved for sinners. In fact, it was such religious people who eventually crucified him, because he dared say that there was a place for them among his friends.

Let us look, briefly, at where this sacrament came from, and how it developed over the years. In the early church, there were people who were guilty of actions that were of such a public nature, that they were a scandal to those who tried to live the gospel message. This would include anything from pagan practices, to denying the promises that went with joining the company of Jesus' followers. Such people were excluded from the Christian community for a certain period of time, until they had a chance to ponder what they had done, and decide if they wished to rejoin the company of believers. Their wrong-doing was of such a public nature, that everybody was aware of it, and the example of their conversion would serve as edification, just as their wrong-doing had served as a scandal. These people became part of what was called the Order of Penitents, and the length of their exclusion varied according to the level of scandal. This was the nearest thing to Confession that existed in the early church. In his letter to the Corinthians, we have Paul calling on them to exclude a man who was giving scandal by his behaviour, and, later on, Paul advises them to re-admit him now into the Christian community.

In the sixth century, Irish monks were involved in what might be described today as spiritual direction, when people called to the monasteries to get advice and counselling. This, in time, developed to a point where sins were mentioned, in the context of things that bothered, and for which advice was needed. This, in turn, led to a prayer over the person, asking for the Lord's forgiveness for any sin involved. The official church of that time strongly opposed this practice, but it persisted, and it was a few centuries later when it was officially recognised as a sacrament. By the time I came along, it had been fine-honed to a ritual of observance and procedure that was detailed down to the last. It had become part of 'pure' religion, where the emphasis was on law, rather than love. When so much emphasis was put on what we did, and when the human input took over in importance, it had wandered far from the idea of Incarnation, where God came to meet us, in our brokenness. Once again, the divine initiative had been turned into human endeavour. There was also another dimension that crept in, that must be acknowledged. After the Reformation, the Roman Catholic Church became even more entrenched in the correctness of what it taught, and if the Protestants dared suggest that there was forgiveness available in any other way, Confession was re-emphasised as being the way to be reconciled to the Lord. That anyone should suggest that salvation was a free gift, was totally unacceptable to those who were fully committed to getting it together through definite and correct procedures. In this, I believe that the church lost its way, but I must be fair in trying to understand how, and why, this had happened. I believe that this was but one of many ways in which the emphasis shifted, and it must be seen against the background of the times. When I was a lad, we had several very serious 'sins' that are not considered to be sins at all now. In my home diocese, we had two reserved sins, forgiveness for which was reserved to the bishop, … making poteen (distilled spirits), and going to dances during Lent. Now, we may well laugh at that today, and see it for what it really was, but, at the time, such things were considered unbecoming, and it does not seem to have caused any great problem that a bishop could add a few more sins to the list, if he thought fit to do so. In our own day, it is relatively recently that we are beginning to recognise that tax evasion, and fiddling the dole, are wrong, and within the sin bracket. The big sin in today's world, is that half the world is dying of hunger, while the other half is on a diet, trying to get down the weight. It is true to say that injustice and wrong-doing are greatly influenced and effected by the times, places, and circumstances in which they occur. I am not at all advocating some sort of situation ethic, where the situation determines whether something is right or not. Murder is murder, and sin is sin, but there are degrees of gravity. Making poteen could hardly be termed a sin, but, the destruction that can happen in a family, as a result of alcoholism can be positively evil. It is too simplistic to generalise and list particular acts as sins, without considering the motive behind the action, and the results of the action, which can deeply effect the gravity, or otherwise of the action. I think it is important to take as broad a view as possible, and to inform and form one's conscience with all the elements in place. Even acts that are good in themselves, can be evil, if the motive is not good. I could visit someone in hospital, which can be a good act, but I'm doing so with a view to regaling my pals with lurid details of the unfortunate's predicament. I could do a good act, for a very wrong reason. I could do many kind acts, because I am looking for votes in an election, and I could attend Mass for the purpose of making someone else look bad. In other words, it is not just black and white, and the approach of the past basically said that it was.

I do believe in the sacrament of Reconciliation, but not as I experienced it, as I grew up. Today, during Advent and Lent, we have services of Reconciliation, and I must confess that I delight in those, and am grateful to have lived to witness this development. There is a community dimension to sin, that must be stressed. When I visit a shopping complex to make a few purchases, I can be sure than my movements are being monitored on a television screen, and store detectives are watching my every move. More than likely, there is a little added to the prices I will be charged, to make up the short-fall, resulting from shop-lifting. Now, I can very well protest that I have not been involved in such behaviour, but I am paying for the behaviour of others. There are areas in a city where public transport is curtailed after certain hours, and people, entirely innocent, are suffering because of the sins of others. It is only correct, therefore, that reconciliation take place within the context of the community, rather than being confined to the secrecy of a confessional. The confessional has its place, and there will always be need for individual confession, but I do not believe that this should be the norm. In a programme like the Twelve Steps of Alcoholics Anonymous, it is strongly advocated that a personal moral inventory of my life, which is then shared with another, is a necessary step towards clearing the wreckage of the past. This is a once-off undertaking, if properly carried out, and is followed by daily checking on my behaviour, and, if I am wrong, I promptly admit it. This has more to do with recon-ciliation with myself and with others, than about any alien-ation from God. The alcoholic has been in the grips of self-will run riot, and it is only the daily dose of truth, that in-cludes admission of guilt when necessary, that will serve as an antidote to that. Facing up to the deceits I find within my-self, and in my behaviour, is the perfect antibiotic for the in-fections of selfishness and self-will. I don't see Confession, as in former times, being very helpful or healing in a recovery process. It had far too much to do with guilt-tripping, and self-recrimination, something that was often made worse by a less than Christ-like attitude of the confessor. Only God is constant, the same yesterday, today, and always. Nothing else can remain the same, and everything else in always in the process of change and evolution. For example, Religious Life, as in nuns, monks, brothers, etc, as we knew it, is finished, and we are now experimenting with new ways of developing and living it. The country-side is dotted with the ruins of old monasteries, and that was what was there before Religious life, as we have known it. I also believe that, in the same way, Confession, as I knew it, growing up, is finished, and we now have to experiment with new ways of celebrating our reconciliation with God, and coming back to the baptismal font, to start again. I believe that the fall-off in the use of Confession might well have less to do with people losing a sense of sin, than of God's Spirit renewing his church, and bringing us into a renewed awareness of the message of the gospel.

No matter what form this reconciliation takes in the future, there will always be a need for on-going reconciliation with God, and with others. When I was a lad, we had a wireless, which was run on batteries. It was never very reliable, and one of my memories is that it had a kind of drifting dial, which caused it to drift off the station from time to time, and someone always had to be on stand-by, to tune it back on the station again. Another memory I have from childhood involves sitting in a train, on my way to Dublin, looking out the window, and being fascinated by the telegraph wires that kept going out of sight at each pole, and then sagging between the poles. Both images help us see what normally happens in our lives. We can drift, and sag, in the normal course of events, and, unless we do something to correct this, we can easily slip and slip, until we are totally down. A sacrament is a decision, and it includes the grace or power to carry out the decision. John and Mary could decide to live together, or they could come to church, and sacramentalise that decision. Now they have the grace of the sacrament in living out the commitment. A sacrament has much more to do with the future, than with the past. I am a priest, and if someone comes to me for Confession, I am more interested in hearing what is going to happen after that person has gone out the door, than anything that may have happened before he entered. If it's just forgiveness of sins I am looking for, then Jesus said that if I forgive, I am forgiven. Confession is not about changing yesterday. 'Lord, give the serenity to accept the things I cannot change...' If, however, I want to change to-morrow, and make sure that it's not just a repeat of yesterday, then, I would argue, I need the sacrament to enable me do this. In the past, many people went to confession trying to change yesterday, which was seen as wiping the slate, making sure that all records were cleared. I would suggest that I should go to the sacrament of Reconciliation, when I am ready to change to-morrow, and I come asking for the power to do so. The decision about to-morrow comes out of yesterday's sins, of course, but this attitude ensures that I am looking forward, and not backward. 'Lord, give me also, the courage to change the things I can, and the wisdom to know the difference.'

I'm sorry if this chapter has been somewhat heavy, and I don't think I told a story at all throughout. I think that this is very very important, and I am anxious that we should give serious consideration to the points raised. I am also severely limited by space, while not wishing to be too skimpy in my treatment of particular points. Forgiveness of others is the key to receiving forgiveness myself There is no such thing as a magic formula in this, and there is nothing automatic about it. If I wrote out every sin I ever committed, translated them into several languages, illustrated them with diagrams, went to Rome, and got absolution from the Pope in ten languages, there is not one of my sins forgiven, if I have unforgiveness in my heart towards another human being. On the other hand, if I am forgiving towards others, and am ready to come before the Lord to ask his forgiveness, then I am always in the mainstream of reconciliation. I remember some years ago, when the Irish soccer team first created a stir on the European football scene, I was visiting a man who was dying of cancer, but who still had enough energy to be intensely interested in each game, as it came along. He would be propped up in bed, and would not miss a kick of the ball, from start to finish. Some weeks after the championship was over, I visited with him, and he was now very weak, and unable to sit up, or to take any interest in football. He was asking me about death and dying, and I was sharing with him what I believe happens at that time. I used the following imagery: Jesus could very well sit me down in front of a huge video screen, and put on a video called 'This is your life'. I could be quite uncomfortable, watching this, until I begin to notice blanks occurring here and there. As my life unfolds, the blanks become more frequent, and, when, eventually, I ask him for an explanation of the blanks, he tells me that these were times when I did something wrong, and then I admitted it. He then pressed the erase button, and it was gone, and, even now, if I asked him what those things were, he would not be able to remember. When God forgives, he suffers from total amnesia. I must say that I am delighted that, when I die, I will be judged by God. I wouldn't trust people at all!

7 Playing God

Religion comes from the Latin word *religare*, and it literally means to be bound to a set of rules or obligations. It is basically external, in that it has to do with external practice. It is very important that I explain exactly what I mean here. If I could draw a line down the middle of a page, with the word Religion at the top of one column, and Spirituality at the top of the other, and drew a contrast between them, comparing one side with the other, it would be clearer what I am trying to say. What I am doing now, however, is speaking about religion on its own, and then, in the next chapter, speaking about spirituality. Because the word religion is generally used in the context of Catholic religion, Protestant religion, etc, and I come across as being anti-religion, you may be confused. I am not thinking Catholic, Protestant, or denomination of any type, when I use the word. What I mean are the things we do, and the practices we perform, as religious people, and where those external practices are given an importance that they do not merit or deserve. I will be stressing that it is the spirit which inspires the practice that gives it any value, and never the practice by itself.

To understand religion, we must go back to the time of Moses, and the Ten Commandments. Moses wrote that if a person could be perfectly good all his life, never yield to temptation, and never sin once, that such a person could be saved. That sort of statement frightens me, because there is no one good, but God, as Jesus told the young man in the gospel. Such a standard of behaviour produced an all-out emphasis on law, and on strict observance of law. The Jews had rules, laws, and regulations for every single thing they did, even to the exact number of yards they were allowed walk on a Sabbath day. They had laws about dress, about food, and even about washing their hands. The law was so important to them, that they had an elite group, called the Scribes, whose whole purpose was to interpret the law in its minutest details. They also had a group, called Pharisees, whose task it was to impose the law, and to punish those who failed in any of its observances. They were totally taken up with law, and they saw their whole relationship with God as depending totally on their strict observance. Their God was very much into a love of law, just as Jesus would later stress the law of love. St Paul inherited this, and he tells us that he was one of the most religious persons of his time, and he did everything within his power to keep every minute detail of his religion. When he was converted to Christianity, he would contrast his attitude then, to the new-found freedom he now had, and would see the law for the slavery that it was.

Jesus' strongest condemnations were reserved for religious people. He called them hypocrites, and he said they were like white marble tomb-stones, beautiful on the outside, but full of rottenness underneath. He condemned them for being more interested in a cup being clean on the outside, while, inside it could be dirty, and badly stained. He really drew the anger of religious people, and he knew that they sought every opportunity to oppose him, and trip him up. He frightened them, because if they lost their great emphasis on laws and religious practices, they had no further reason for living. Religious people are totally opposed to change, because, to do so is to admit that what they have been doing up till now was not perfect. There is a degree of insecurity about religious people, because of this fear of change. 'To live is to change, and to become perfect is to have changed often', said Cardinal Newman. We are a pilgrim people, and, just as the scenery and surroundings change, as I travel along on a pilgrimage, so does life, and the way of looking at things. We are in process, in a state of constant change. God is infinite, and at no one point can we say that we know God, or understand him. I am like a tiny fish in the middle of the Atlantic ocean, which is God, and each day I swim around getting new experiences of the same sea. I would be a very foolish little fish, and a very dead little fish, if I attempted to rise above the sea, and get an over-view, from shore to shore. I look out to sea, but I cannot claim to see the water, because all I can see is the top of the water, and not the millions of gallons underneath. Life is a continual path of discovery, and God is constantly revealing himself; and to rise above merely existing, and begin to live, I must always be open to those new revelations of this God of surprises.

Original sin was us humans trying to be as good as God, trying to declare our independence from God. That sin, in a thousand forms, persists to this day. There is some sort of deep-rooted pride within the human psyche, and it is dangerous and destructive. I remember a phrase of my father's, when I was a lad, and when I stepped out of line. 'You don't seem to know your place. Some day I'm going to put you in your place.' I never knew exactly what he meant, but I knew I had over-stepped my limits, and was out of bounds, as far as he was concerned. I have often thought of that since, when I reflect on how we can attempt to run the show for God, and to step into areas which are away beyond our limits. Evil is most evil when it is disguised as good, and surely the self-righteous parading of religion as virtue is a travesty. If I really knew my place before God, and how wide the gap is, I would surely fall on my face, and wouldn't dare raise my eyes. That God should condescend to join me on the journey of life, and that he should call me friend, is extraordinary; but that I should expect God to take a back seat, while I show him how perfect I am; that I should expect him to shut up and listen while I tell him all I am doing for him; that I should expect him to pin a medal on me, and thank me for being so good, ... that is religion at its most obnoxious level. The Pharisees disgusted Jesus, because there is no way they were prepared to listen. Jesus tells a story of a Pharisee who went up to the temple to pray. (In fact, in another context, Jesus said that they made sure they prayed in very public places, so that people would see them.) They laid great importance on parading their virtue. Anyhow, back to the Pharisee in the temple. Jesus said that 'he stood up, and prayed thus to himself'. Notice, he was not praying to God, because God, and everyone else around, was supposed to be silent, and listen to what he had to say. Instead of 'Praise the Lord', he was more into 'Praise me Lord'. Religion, without the inner spirit, is an empty shell, and, as St Paul would put it, sounding brass and clanging cymbals.

Let me try to be more specific in what I am saying. Depending on the observance of laws, rules, and regulations, to make me right with God, and to earn my salvation, is wrong, wrong, wrong. I cannot earn or merit anything from God, or anything that is of God. It is total gift. Laws can be good, they can be helpful. Speed limits for cars travelling through a town is a wise safeguard, but, as with an ambulance, with flashing light, and screeching siren, there are times when such laws must be put aside, for a greater good. Pure religion, as practised and promoted by the Pharisees, allowed for no exceptions. At that point, it becomes enslavement, and ridiculous. Jesus was strongly reprimanded for healing someone, because it was the Sabbath, and he should do nothing on that day of rest! This would be funny, if it wasn't really sad. The unfortunate thing about all of this is that a lot of it has survived over the years even though Jesus had died to bring us across a bridge from a love of law into a law of love.

The church I grew up in, had, to a large extent, gone back over that bridge again into a love of law. My catechism was chock-full of rules and regulations. I had commandments coming out of my ears. By then, we had added the commandments and precepts of the church to the Ten

Commandments. The conditions for proper reception of sacraments, for obtaining indulgences, for obtaining forgiveness of sin, were down to such detail, that the strictest Pharisee would have felt totally at home in the church, and, indeed, Jesus could well have felt that he didn't belong there. I remember hearing a story about a black man, and a whites-only church, in one of the southern states of the United States. It was a Sunday morning, and the service was in full swing, and the black man was standing outside, listening to the music, because, of course, he was not allowed go in. After a while Jesus came along, and began to talk to him. He asked him why he had not gone inside to the service, and the man said that he had tried, but was unable to gain admission. Jesus smiled, and said 'Don't worry. I know how you feel. I myself have been trying to get into that church for years!'

I often think of Pope John XXIII falling on his knees, and asking for another Pentecost, because we had blown that last one. I believe we then got another Pentecost, and we are now in the process of bringing the church back over the bridge into the law of love. It's a tough haul, because, like Jesus in his day, religious people find it very hard to change. If some people had their way, we would still have the Latin Mass, and there certainly would not be guitars in church! In a world of hungry people, that anyone in the church should make an issue out of guitars in church, or girl Mass servers, is obscene and pathetic. As I said in an earlier chapter, religion can be frightening, because it can put rules and regulations in front of the welfare of people. The ideals that Hitler held, were more important to him than the welfare of millions. OK, the church doesn't burn people at the stake anymore, but there's more than one way to skin a cat. On a regular basis, we read in our papers where baptism is refused because the parents are not married, or are not regular church goers. I respectfully suggest we leave all judgements to God, and try to extend Christ's love and acceptance to those we meet. Who am I to say that this child will not grow into the fullness of the gospel message, or that my non-judgmental acceptance of the parents might not be a moment of grace for them, to motivate them to look again at what they may have rejected. I have known some priests who have been so legalistic and bureaucratic about preparation for marriage, that I would not at all blame the couple, if they went to the nearest registry office. I am not suggesting that we should ignore all rules. Far from it. I am saying, however, that the church should be seen to be more on the side of the welfare of people than strict adherence to law. The compassion of Jesus must always be put before and above all rules.

I heard of a man at a prayer meeting, who confessed that he had been a wife-beater, a child molester, and that he had been involved in robbery with violence. 'However,' he said, 'I want to thank the Lord here to-night that, throughout all that time, I never lost my religion.' Whenever I watch movies like The Godfather, I am always upset to see how the most callous mobster, with blood on his hands, is seen to be in church on all the significant occasions. This is not as far-fetched as it seems. I could well have more to answer for, on the day of judgement, for my attendance at church, than for the times I did not attend. I believe that religious practices, not based on sincerity, and inspired by God's Spirit, must be an abomination in the sight of the Lord.

Ecumenism, or the coming together of the Christian churches, can be greatly hindered by religion, where the emphasis is on uniformity, rather than unity. Religion is, essentially, about conformity, and it does not allow for such things as personal revelation, or divine inspiration, on a personal level. Many of our greatest saints were badly treated by the institutional church, because they dared be different. St Francis was considered a nuisance, and a dreamer, while Joan of Arc was a dangerous revolutionary. The divisions among the Christian churches is a scandal, and a sad example to the world of the religious subversion of a message of love, toleration, and forgiveness that was preached by the one whom

each church would claim as founder. All of this is the outcome of religion holding sway over spirituality, and rigid adherence to rule and tradition holding sway over the all-em-
bracing love and compassion of Jesus Christ. There must be a
place within the church for a very wide spectrum, indeed,
but, unfortunately, the use of anathemas, and excommunica-
tions, issued by self-righteous bigots, who were so sure of
their own monopoly on truth, led to a level of intolerance that
totally betrayed the mind of Jesus. Thankfully, to a large extent, we are growing into a humbler church. We are channels
of the Lord's healing love, not generators of his power.

The story is told of a secondary teacher who died, and appeared at the gate of heaven. As he tried to enter, St Peter
stopped him, and explained that they were operating a
points system, and, at present it was one thousand points for
entry. Peter asked him what he had done during his life-time,
to which the teacher replied, with appropriate emphasis, that
he had been to Mass every morning, for fifty years. Peter was
duly impressed, and announced 'OK, that's one point.' The
poor teacher was badly taken aback, because he had spent
much time and energy preparing just for this moment. Peter
asked him what else he had done, and he replied that he had
been involved in fund-raising for charitable organisations.
When he was asked how much money was involved, he
shoved out his chest, as he announced that he had raised over
thirty thousand pounds. Peter said that was very good, and
that was another point! The poor man was shattered, and he
muttered to himself 'It's only by the grace of God that I'm
going to get in there.' Peter heard him, turned to him, and
said, 'If you really believe that it is only by the grace of God
you are going to get in there, go on in, because that, my
friend, is the thousand points.' There is no place for members
of the white-knuckle club, or for muscular Christianity
among the followers of Jesus Christ. Remember what I said,
at the beginning, about Moses, and the perfect observance of
rules and regulations that he advocated for salvation. Well,

Jesus has changed all that completely, and for ever. It is total gift, and cannot be merited or earned. If I prayed and fasted for the rest of my life, I wouldn't earn one iota of salvation. In a later chapter I will speak of prayer, and the place it has in our journey with the Lord. Notice I did not say towards the Lord, because, as a result of Incarnation, the Lord is travelling with us. When I speak of prayer, I will speak more about listening than speaking, because prayer is really what God does, when I stop talking, and start listening. I will speak about a spirituality of subtraction, rather than one of addition, when, like John the Baptist, I begin to decrease in my own importance, so that the Lord can increase. St Paul said that, if he boasted, he boasted in the Lord, because, he himself had nothing of which he could boast. A frog, living in a forest in New Jersey, persuaded two geese to fly him to Florida for the winter. He tied the ends of a long cord to each goose, he held the centre of the cord in his mouth, and off they went to Florida. The journey was going well until someone on the ground noticed the strange sight passing by overhead. 'Hey, look at that!', he shouted, 'that's fantastic. Whose idea was that, I wonder?' In his anxiety to get the credit for being so clever, the proud frog opened his mouth, and shouted 'Mine!' Humility, and profound gratitude is the only fitting response to the love that is offered. To try to run the show, to reverse the roles, and have God under an obligation to us for being so good, is a pathetic distortion of his plan of salvation for us.

In the following chapter I will speak about Spirituality, which is what God effects in us, and through us, when we let him. Religion has had more to do with maintenance than with mission, with controlling than with confirming, and, through its involvement with earthly powers over the centuries, with conquering and capturing than with captivating. Religion is about control, while Spirituality is about surrender. Religion is what we do, while Spirituality is about what God does. Pure religion can be nothing more than original sin, dressed up as virtue, where we are trying to be as good as

God. I believe that Christianity is, essentially, about attracting, rather than promoting. God becomes God in my life, the
very moment I stop playing God. God is love, and
Christianity is based on the law of love, and it is by this witness alone that Jesus said we are to be recognised as his disciples.

8 Letting go

According to the story of creation, God took clay, and formed it into a particular shape, and then he breathed his spirit into it, and it became alive, and the first human was created. Now, I am not at all saying that that was how it actually happened, all I need know is that God created people, and that, yes, it was his breath that was passed on to them to give them life. Breath is highlighted as being very important from the beginning of creation. Obviously, breath is important, anyhow, because the first and last thing we do when we enter and leave this world is take a breath. That first breath sets the engine going, and that last breath switches off the engine. It is very significant, therefore, that when we got it all wrong, and God decided to re-create us, that he should breathe upon us, once again. 'Jesus breathed on them, and said "Receive the Holy Spirit…"'

It is the spirit within or behind an action that gives it meaning, and prevents it being a shallow, meaningless exercise. I meet people who ask me how I am, and I tell them that I'm OK, because I know that is all they want to hear. I meet others who ask me the exact same question, and I could take several minutes answering their question. It is not the question, but the spirit in the question, that makes all the difference. I could call you a total idiot today, and you could consider me really funny, while, to-morrow, I could call you a total idiot, and you would be deeply offended. It is not the comment, but the spirit that inspires it, that really matters. Spirit is very important, because it is spirit that gives life to words and actions. When you come across a violent mob, who may not actually be involved in violent actions just now, you are, nevertheless, very frightened, because you sense a spirit of anger and destruction among them. Whatever spirit is within is always shown by the words and actions that come out. A man may say he is not angry, but, as you watch him slamming the door, and giving the dog a kick, you have good reason to doubt his assertion. Religion might be described as goodness, without a good spirit. It is not life-giving, because, unless the spirit and breath of God inspires my words and actions, they cannot give life.

The prophet Ezekiel had a vision, in which he was taken into a valley full of dry bones. God asked the prophet if these bones could live again, and he replied, 'Lord, only you know that.' God then asked him to speak to the bones, and say to them 'I am going to put my spirit in you, and you shall live.' Ezekiel then called on the bones to come together, which they did. Then they were covered with flesh, and finally, with skin. Then God said to the prophet 'Speak on my behalf, and call on the Spirit ... Say to the Spirit: "Come from the four winds. Breathe into these dead bones, and let them live."' The prophet did as God asked, and breath entered the bodies ... 'they came alive, standing on their feet – a great, immense army.' God went on to explain to the prophet that the vision was a symbol of what he was going to do for his people, who were spiritually dead. God said he would open their graves, breathe his Spirit into them, and they would become alive again. In this, we see that God himself thought of re-creating as breathing his Spirit once again into the clay of our beings. That Spirit would be God's power and life within us, and, when we live by that power, and when we speak and act in full awareness of that inner power, I am calling that Spirituality.

Do you remember, in the first chapter of this book when I spoke of the raisins in the dough, and the scone that is allocated to each one of us? Jesus was anointed and empowered with the Spirit, when he came up out of the river Jordan, at his baptism. With that power within him, he took on all our human weaknesses, one after another, and overcame them. He proved once for all that God's power was much stronger than all human weaknesses put together. Now he gives us back the scone, which still has our own quota of weaknesses in it, but he also offers us his Spirit, so that we will have more than enough power to deal with those weaknesses. The Holy Spirit, which Jesus offers us, is like Popeye's spinach, that enables us do things that are away beyond us. The most important condition for receiving this power is that I am convinced I really need it. One time there was a crow, that was very depressed, down-in-the-mouth, and with feathers all droopy and dishevelled. His friends were really worried about him, so three of them came to visit him, to find out what was wrong. The crow was hesitant at the beginning, insisting that all was well, but, eventually, he came around to talking about what was troubling him. He considered himself a great failure in life, because he had but a few ambitions, and now life was passing him by, and he had achieved nothing. When one of them asked him what his ambitions were, he was really embarrassed, but confessed that his big ambition was to make a record. Trying to suppress a smile, one of the other crows asked what would he have done on the record, and he replied 'Singing, of course.' At this point, one of his visitors lost control, and laughed out loud. This really upset our friend, who became highly indignant, and really angry. 'Why couldn't I sing? Did you ever hear a blackbird sing? Well, I'm the same colour, and I'm bigger. Why couldn't I sing like a blackbird? If you only knew the trouble I have gone to, to be able to sing like a blackbird. I went to a health shop, where I got wholegrain seeds, vivioptol, royal jelly, and the whole collection of health products that would improve my general well-being. After all that, I flew up on a tree, and began to sing, but all I could say was "Caw! Caw!" I then bought a tape-recorder, put a C-90 tape in it, and flew up among the blackbirds, and filled the tape with the sounds of the black-

birds singing. Then I bought a walkman, and with the head-
phones on my head, I lay back, and listened to the singing
day and night. This way, I was sure I could learn to sing like a
blackbird. However, when I flew back up on the tree again,
and attempted to sing, all I could produce was just more
"Caw! Caw!" I was really depressed, so I tried something
else. This time, I bought sheet music, and went for voice-
training. I spent a lot of time and money on this, and, again,
to no avail. All I had to show for it was more of the "Caw!
Caw!" By this time, I was really in the depths of despair.'

At this point the poor crow just walked away and left his
friends, because recounting his litany of failures was just too
much for him. It was months later when they all met up
again, and, this time, things had changed totally. When his
friends asked him what had happened, he told them: 'One
morning, as I returned from my morning flying exercise, I
was glancing through the paper, when lo and behold, I read
about a doctor in South Africa, called Christian Bernard, who
did transplants. My heart missed a beat with the excitement,
as I thought I had found the solution to my problem. This
was it. A transplant. I got on the phone, and phoned South
Africa, and got the doctor, and asked him what kind of transplants he did. When he told me about heart, lung, and liver
transplants, I asked him if he ever did voice-box transplants.
No, he said, he had never done one of those. I asked if he
would consider doing one, and he said it should be much
easier than a heart transplant, and it was surely possible to do
one. I asked if I might come to see him, and he invited me to
South Africa. I arrived there some time later, and waited, as
he got in touch with local hospitals, and mortuaries, waiting
for a blackbird that had just passed away, … especially one
with a donor card! Eventually, a voice-box became available,
and everything was set up for the operation. I put myself in
his hands, and told him to go ahead with the transplant. The
operation was a success, and I now had the voice-box of a
blackbird. When I had fully recovered, I flew up on a tree,

and began to practise with my new voice-box, and, in no time at all, I was singing away like a blackbird, with the best of them. I also came to realise that, because of what had happened, I could never sing any other way again. It was only then it dawned on me that I had been very very foolish all over the years, because I had been trying to sing like a blackbird, without having what it takes to do so. I do not regret all the trouble and expense I went to, however, because I believe that if I hadn't tried all those things, I would never have discovered that they just didn't work.' And, that, my friend, is the secret of Spirituality. Religion is working within the limits of what I have, and trying to get it together on my own. Spirituality is getting a transplant, and using my new-found gift to do things that I never could have done by myself.

A heart transplant takes place in two distinct stages. Firstly the old defective heart has to be removed. The patient must agree to this, and sign a paper giving permission for this to happen. Even prior to that must be a clear medical diagnosis that the old heart is of no further use, and is no longer capable of fulfilling the function for which it was created. The second part of the operation is to implant a new heart. Unfortunately, for this to happen, someone must die. The prophets in the Old Testament, that part of the Bible that tells us what happened before Jesus came, these prophets talk about a saviour coming to redeem us, and that he would take out our heart of stone, and give us a heart of flesh. In other places, the prophets speak of God putting a new spirit in us, and making us new again. Once again, someone had to die for this to take place. I believe the very highest point of what Jesus made possible for us, through his death, was that he could give us his Spirit, so that we could live with his power, and share in his life. He told the apostles that, when the Spirit came, they would do even greater things than he did. In offering us his Spirit, Jesus is offering us nothing less than a full sharing in his own life. There was a family that had fallen on hard times. The family business had failed, and they lost everything they had. The neighbours came to the father to enquire if they could do anything to help, and he said that he would love to take his wife and children, get away from it all, and settle somewhere in America, where no one would know them, and they could start afresh. The neighbours organised several fund-raising ventures, and, after several months, they gave the father the tickets for the boat trip from Cobh to New York. The family had never been out of the country before, and had no idea how to prepare for such a voyage. They bought bread, last week's bread, which was stale but cheap, and, with lettuce and cheese, they made sandwiches, a whole lot of sandwiches, which they packed in boxes, and brought with them on board. They gathered together in a single cabin, resolved to stay to themselves throughout the voyage. On the first, second, third, fourth, fifth day, when they were hungry they ate sandwiches. On the sixth, seventh, eighth day, the bread was really hard, and the cheese began to smell, and they were in a sad way. One day, with a few days left before arriving in New York, one little lad was crying, and he begged his parents to give him a penny or two, so that he could go up on deck and buy a few sweets. The father gave him a few pence, and off he went. It was over an hour later, and he had not returned, and his family was really worried about him. Finally, the father had to come out of his cabin, and go in search of the lad. When he came up on deck, he was shocked to see his son, with many other people, all sitting around a long table, and each with a plate of meat, vegetables, and potatoes. He noticed that his son was totally immersed in the food, and he had a large glass of coke in front of him. The father came up behind him, nudged him in the back, and whispered 'Why did you do this? You know we cannot afford this', to which the boy replied, with eyes sparkling, and mouth full, 'Ah, but daddy, we could have had this all the time. This was included with the tickets.' I often imagine people dying, going to heaven, and expressing delight and amazement at the beauty and luxury of it all, and Jesus saying to

them, 'But you could have had this all the time, this was included with the tickets. I offered you life in abundance, my
peace, my joy, and my Spirit, and, in spite of all that, you insisted on settling for sandwiches, when I invited you to the
fullness of the banquet.' I believe that the road to heaven is
heaven, just as the road to hell is hell. I believe that I will get
nothing when I die that I am not offered now. Unfortunately,
people who do not have the right attitude to be open to Jesus
and his message, seem to think that the road to heaven is hell,
and the road to hell is heaven.

Christianity is something that happens inside, when the
Spirit comes, and Incarnation takes place within me. Like
Mary, Jesus is formed in me, and I become another Christ.
God created us in his image, and it is the work of the Spirit to
bring forth that image in us. A young lad was passing the
sculptor's workshop one morning, when he noticed a huge
lump of marble, awaiting the sculptor's chisel. Each morning
after that, as the boy passed by, the door of the workshop was
closed, but he could hear the sounds of work going on inside.
Finally, one morning, as he went to school, the door was open
wide, and the boy looked in, and there, where the marble had
been, was a huge life-like statue of a tiger. The boy was awe-
struck by the sheer beauty and power of the statue. He went
into the workshop, went up to the sculptor, pulled his sleeve,
and asked 'Excuse me, sir, but how did you know that there
was a tiger in there?' It is the work of the Spirit to reveal what
is within. Religion is about externals, and is involves things
we do. Spirituality is internal, and it is purely the work of
God's Spirit. As I write now, I have just made a decision. If
it's OK with you, I would like to finish this chapter with a
prayer, in which I will pray for an outpouring of the Spirit
upon you. That will be at the end, and we're not there yet. I
just thought I should share that with you in advance.

My openness to the Spirit is in direct proportion to my
awareness of my own weaknesses. If there were no weaknesses, there would be no need of the power, and there

would be no witness value to our lives. The greatest witness a
recovering alcoholic can give, is to walk, sober, down the
main street of his local town. His brother, who never touched
alcohol in his life, would be unable to give the same witness,
because he does not have the same weakness. If you could
imagine a light-house, at night time. A powerful light shines
out, that is seen for miles around, yet the same light is being
attacked by thousands upon thousands of flying creatures, all
attracted by it. The very weakness that attracts the temptation, is the very same weakness that must give witness to the
light. Like the raisins in the scone, I have my human weaknesses, and they will never go away, and will always be part
of who and what I am. With the power of the Spirit within,
however, I am able to act above, and in spite of those weaknesses, and it is this very evidence that witnesses to the presence of a Higher Power within. The alcoholic is always an alcoholic, even fifty years after taking his last drink. Jesus said to
his apostles 'Very soon now, you will receive power from on
high, and you will be my witnesses to the ends of the earth.'
With the privilege of power, goes the responsibility of witnessing. No weakness, no witness. That is why St Paul said
that where he was weak was exactly where he had become
strong, because the power of God is seen to greater effect in
human weakness.

Religion is about control, while spirituality is about surrender. It is about getting out of the way, and letting God be
God in my life. This decision comes from deep within, from
that part of me where I am most authentic. The human soul is
like a deep deep well, that, as life goes on, tends to get filled
up with all kinds of junk and garbage. The Greek word for
conversion is called kinosis, which, literally, means to empty
out. Conversion is about dumping the garbage, so that, the
more I get rid of, the more clear water from the deep well can
come to the surface. Jesus said that the Sprit rises up from
within a person. In other words, the Spirit rises up from the
heart to the head, as something that is experienced first, and,

perhaps, understood later. Comparing the Spirit to a spring of living water rising up from within us, is Jesus' way of referring to a very special kind of thirst we have, that can never be quenched in any other way. A young lad went to a wise old monk, one time, and said he was looking for God, and he wanted to know where he would find him. The old monk brought him down to the river, put him in the water, and held his head under the water, until he nearly drowned. When the monk lifted the lad's head up out of the water, his gasp of air could be heard a good distance away. Then the old monk said to him 'When you want God as much as you wanted that breath of air, you will find him.'

And now, I would like to lead you in that prayer I referred to earlier. There is no magic formula. It is never the words, but the spirit in the words. God is more interested in what my heart is doing than what my lips are saying, when I pray. If you really want to receive his spirit, then be sure that you will. OK, let's begin. Heavenly Father, I thank you for the plan of salvation you offered us in Jesus. Thank you, Father, for wanting us back in your family, and for wanting to share your life with us. Jesus said that you would surely give your Spirit to those who ask, and so, in Jesus' name, I ask you, please, to release the power and fullness of your Spirit within my heart. Fill every corner of my being with the power and healing light of your Spirit. Jesus, thank you for making all this possible. I want to thank you in the best possible way, and that is by opening my heart wide to all that you died to be able to offer me. Spirit, breath, and power of God, please make your home within me, in my own personal Pentecost of love and understanding. Come with your gifts, to empower me to live with the life of God, with a whole new courage, and generosity, and with an experience of the everyday presence of God on every step of life's journey. Amen.

9 Pie in the sky

Heaven is a state of being, rather than some place to which we go. It is being in God, and living with him, and allowing him live in me. What makes heaven so mysterious is, that we think of it as something that comes after we die. I think that is a great mistake. There is nothing I will get when I die that I am not offered now. The difference between now and hereafter, is that the struggle will be over, the tensions will be gone, the weeds among the wheat will be burned, and I will have arrived. I will have arrived where? I will have arrived as good wheat in the store-house of the Lord, as part of a harvest that is saved, and that can no longer be choked with weeds, or flattened by wind and rain. The wheat won't be any better than it was before the harvest; it will, however, be safer. Please remember that the struggles and the tensions are good, because that's what life is. If God gave me a choice of perfection now, I would turn it down flat, because I would have no further reason to live. Any compassion and empathy I have has come out of my struggles with my own brokenness, and any worthwhile growth in my life has always been at times of conflict. If I really took the Lord seriously, and came to believe his promises, I would see my life now as being full of opportunities, rather than burdened with problems. To the fool every opportunity is a problem, but to the wise every problem is an opportunity.

We go back to the raisins in the scone again. Of course, there are weaknesses, but, a million times more important than that is the power that is made available to me. As the children today sing, as part of the First Communion programme, 'Ooh, ooh, ooh, ooh, heaven is in my heart.' Wouldn't it be wonderful if these children believed that, and did not think of heaven as something that happens after we die? And especially as something that I have to spend my life earning, and saving up for! This is like re-inventing the wheel, as if Jesus hasn't done enough to bring heaven down here among us. When Jesus went down into the Jordan river, we are told that the heavens opened, the Father's voice was heard, and the Spirit came upon Jesus in visible form. When Jesus bowed his head on Calvary, the veil of the temple was torn in two, the veil that separated the people from the Holy of Holies, which was thought of as being the dwelling of God. From that moment, as St Paul says, we can come boldly into the presence of God, assured of his acceptance, because of what Jesus Christ has done for us. In the Mass we say 'Lord, by your cross and resurrection, you have set us free. You are the saviour of the world.' Would that we really believed that! If we believed that, we would not be working our tails off to earn or merit something that is ours already, if we would only accept it. I would strongly argue that my Christian vocation has nothing to do with getting to heaven, but has everything to do with getting heaven down here. I often think that it is much more difficult to get heaven into people, than to get people into heaven.

Let me return, for a moment, to the struggles, tensions, and failures that are part of our journey on this earth. Have you ever examined a tapestry from both sides? On top, it is a work of art, and a joy to behold. Underneath, there's neither beginning nor end to it, with wool, and bits of twine going all over the place. That's our view of life, and, I believe that God has a very different view. God sees from above, we can only see from below. Imagine, if you can, a huge oil painting stretching the length of a wall, and the scene is one of extraordinary beauty. Now cover the painting with a cloth, and cut out a small hole in the cloth, to reveal just a tiny part of the scenery. That's my view of the over-all scene. At death, the cloth is whipped away, and the full scene is unveiled. What I had been able to see is still there, but, it is now part of the complete picture, and I see it as something that is very much part of a much bigger scene. I am now like someone standing in a large cardboard box, and I cannot see out over the sides of the box. At death, the sides of the box fall away, and I look around, with a gasp of wonder, at the vast expanse of beauty that surrounds me, something that had been there all the time, but, with the limitations of my humanity, I was unable to even imagine. What I am saying is that it is all here now, even if I cannot see it. When I look into the distance, I cannot see beyond the horizon, even though I know there is so much more out there. If I look at the ocean I can see only the top of the water, and not the millions of gallons underneath. I share the limitations with my fellow-travellers, even though we all know there is much more to it than that.

Life, now, is living within the limits. Life, for us, is to live the now fully, and leave the future to the Lord. I need never worry what the future holds, if I believe that the Lord holds the future. Jesus has come among us, to walk the journey with us, and he is most insistent in telling us that he will never abandon us, or desert us in the storm. So much of the gospel stories have to do with my journey now, than with the lives of people then. I remember crossing the Sea of Galilee, with a group, and we stopped the boat, and spent about two hours reflecting on passages from the gospels. Those passages were about storms, about terror, about panic, and about fishing all night, without success. It brought the gospel very much alive and present for us all. The gospel is now, and I am every person in the gospel.

I cannot emphasise enough that the struggles, tensions, and failures of life are the very things that make life worthwhile. Without these, I would have no compassion, empathy, or sense of fellowship with those with whom I travel the journey of life. I honestly believe that, viewed from beyond the gates of death, these same struggles and failures will be seen very differently from how they may appear now. A young

lad found a caterpillar in his back garden, and when someone
told him that it would break out of its covering, and, eventually,
become a butterfly, he decided that he could assist it in the
process. So he broke open the covering, and released the
caterpillar from within, and, of course, it promptly shrivelled
up and died. He did not know that the struggle involved in
freeing itself from the crysalis, or covering, was absolutely
necessary for it to have enough strength to fly, and to go on
living. If you ever waken up some morning, and your life is
really together, and the struggles are no more, then, please
don't move … stay where you are, and wait for the undertaker
… because you have arrived at the third and final stage of
life.

St Paul asks the question, 'Having given us Jesus, will the
Father not surely give us everything else?' God will always
provide me with what I need, and, thankfully, not everything
I want. If God was sadistic and cruel, he would grant me
everything I ask, and then have a good laugh, because much
of what I ask for may not be for my good. This man died, and
found himself in a place that seemed quite pleasant. When he
felt hungry, a young lad came in, with a tray of food. When he
felt thirsty, the lad re-appeared with a selection of drinks. As
he grew tired, a bed appeared out of the wall, and he slept. As
time went by, he noticed that, as soon as he felt like something, it was instantly provided. This was very good, for a
while, but, eventually, the whole thing became so predictable
that he was wondering was there going to be any variety in
this kind of life, or was life always going to be more and more
of everything. Finally, one day, he called the young lad, and
asked him if he was ever to be without something in this
place. The lad replied that such would never happen. 'But',
asked the man, 'even things I only half-want, but don't really
need, is that always going to be provided?' 'Oh, yes', replied
the lad. The idea of the day-in day-out predictable nature of
life, did not at all appeal to the man, and he muttered, 'With
life like this, I am beginning to think that I might be better off

in hell', to which the lad replied, 'And where, do you think, you are?'

Religion has always focused our eyes on getting to heaven. It was as if, by sheer volume of prayer and effort, I could build a stairway. We were told that life here is a valley of tears, where we are miserable exiles, and are not supposed to really love this life. I would agree with that idea if I had been in Egypt with the Jews, or been following Moses through the desert for forty years. There was a Promised Land up ahead, and it was towards that my attention would have been directed. I believe that Jesus has changed all of that, and nothing is now the same. Jesus brought heaven down on earth, and the first night he appeared at Bethlehem, the angels came with him. Again, I quote St Paul, who wrote that having given us Jesus won't the Father surely give us everything else? There is a religious science with a big name, called Eschatology. Now Eschatology tells us that what will come, and I am referring to heaven here, is already here, but will be completed later. It speaks of now, but not yet, just as we might sail down a river in a boat, knowing that, eventually, this river will join with the sea, but, like the Gulf Stream in the Atlantic ocean, it will still continue to move, it will still be water. I saw a poster one time which said 'I believe there is a sea, because I have seen a stream.' The real work and function of the stream is what it contributes along its journey; the animals that drink, the land it irrigates, the fish that spawn. The purpose of the stream is not to make the ocean any fuller. Our life is an end in itself, and it must not be dismissed as some sort of Purgatory, which the catechism used define as 'a state or place of punishment, where some souls suffer for a while before they get to heaven.'

I would argue strongly that my life, as a Christian, is to make myself available to the Lord, so that he can continue to get heaven down here. There are people on this earth living in hell, and my role is to bring heaven to them, in any way I can. 'Make me a channel of your peace; where there is hatred, let me bring your love; where there is despair, let me bring your hope, and where there is hunger, let me bring your food.' That, I believe, is my Christian vocation. Religion, that would have me concentrated on making sure I myself got to heaven, would be selfishness of the worst kind. It is not possible to bring light to others, and continue to remain in darkness myself. To refer to another song on the First Communion programme, 'Christ has no body now but yours; no hands, no feet, no voice on earth, but yours.' A group of five men arrived at a railway station, to get a train home, after a business conference. They were rushing across the platform to get on the train, before it pulled out, when one of them accidentally tipped a table with apples on it, where somebody had a stall. One of the other men, who was trying to be a Christian, and who genuinely believed that everybody is important, shouted to the others to go ahead, and he would get the next train. He returned to the stall, to find a ten-year-old boy sitting on a chair beside the apples, and the boy was blind. His mother had gone across to a shop to get something. The man collected the apples that had scattered on the ground, stacked up those that were undamaged, and put some damaged ones to one side. He gave the boy a few dollars to cover the ones that were damaged, and, as he was leaving, he said, 'I'm sorry for what has happened, and I hope we have not spoiled your day.' He had turned away to leave, when the boy whispered to him, 'Excuse me, sir, … but … but … are you Jesus?' And that, my friends, is exactly what my Christian vocation should involve.

While the apostles travelled around with Jesus, they witnessed many wonders, and they heard wonderful news, as they heard him speak. It is extraordinary, therefore, that when they were alone with him, they asked him to teach them to pray. He taught them the 'Our Father'. It is a prayer that is worth reflecting on, because it gives a really good insight into the mind of Jesus. The prayer is really about down here, down here, right now. Even when it does mention heaven, it prays that this might become a reality here among us, where life might become more and more as it is in heaven. In this prayer, we ask God to forgive us as we forgive each other right now, and we ask just for what we need today. On the morning of the Ascension, as Jesus left their sight, the apostles were reminded, quite dramatically, of something Jesus had told them. Two men in brilliant white clothes appeared to them, and asked them why they were looking up to heaven. Jesus had told them very clearly where he was now to be found. He would be found among the hungry, the deprived, the marginalised, and the homeless. In *Cry the Beloved Country*, Alan Paton writes, 'Do not look for me just in sanctuaries, or in the precise words of theologians, or in the calm of the countryside. Look for me in the place where people are struggling for their very survival as human beings.'

A man, who had often wondered what hell and heaven might look like, had a dream one night. In the dream he was firstly brought to see hell. He was very surprised to find that hell consisted of a very large room, with a long table down the centre, and the table was laden down with the most delicious food. What amazed him, however, was that all the people around the table were miserable, and completely malnourished, because each had two five-foot-long chopsticks, and they were not able to get the food up to their mouths. He then was taken to see heaven, and he was even more surprised to find that heaven was also a large room, with a long table down the centre, and the table was laden down with delicious food. Once again, each person had five-foot-long chopsticks, but, things were totally different here, and they all looked very happy and well nourished, as each picked up food with the chopsticks, and fed the person sitting opposite. And that, in a nut-shell is the difference between heaven and hell, and both are available to us here. I don't believe that God sends us anywhere when we die; rather, I think, he eternalises the direction our lives are taking now. I believe that I am to be his touch-person in the lives of others. One of my own favourite prayers is 'Lord, may your Spirit within me touch the hearts of those I meet today, either through the words I say, the prayers I pray, the life I live, or the person I am.' Once again, it is about being a channel of his peace.

Martin Luther King used love to quote 'You write a new page of the gospel each day, by the things that you do, and the words that you say. People read what you write, whether faithful or true. What is the gospel according to you?' Without wishing to hold one church above another, it is accepted that the Protestant churches are seen to be more into evangelising, or preaching the gospel to unbelievers, than the Catholic Church. I believe that this has happened because the Catholic Church has always maintained that its greatest force for evangelising is the example and witness of its members. I always think of Christianity as being more about attracting than promoting, of people asking to join my church, more than me trying to coax them in. If my example doesn't do it, my words certainly won't. The only way this world can become better is when people become better. The best influence I can have in that process is when I myself face up to what, in me, is in need of being redeemed; when I am prepared to name, claim, and tame my own demons. It was a Saturday afternoon, and a father was taking care of his children while his wife had gone shopping. The weather was bad, so they were indoors, and the children were getting under his feet, every time he moved. He decided on a plan to occupy them. He found a magazine, in which there was a map of the world. He got a scissors, and cut the map into many pieces, and gave this to a seven-year-old, as a jig-saw. He then began devising projects for the others. Within about five minutes, he was both surprised and disgusted when he saw that the seven-year-old had completed the jig-saw. He asked him how he had completed the work so quickly, and was surprised to hear the lad say 'Daddy, I didn't know what the world should look like, and I didn't know where to begin. Then I turned over the pieces, and I discovered there was a man on the other side; so when I put the man together, I found that the world was together as well.'

The whole story is all about on-going Incarnation, which continues in and through all of us. In the final analysis, it about being Christ to others, and seeing Christ in others. In the following chapter, I will develop this further, as we look at how we can do this. Once I come to believe that, because of what Jesus has done, I am saved, then it becomes important for me to begin to look saved! When I leave all of the future in the Lord's hands, and come back into today, I begin to give this day all that I have. It is only when I experience reconciliation within my own life, that I can begin to be an instrument of reconciliation in the lives of others. Another song I like is 'Let there be peace on earth, and let it begin with me.'

10 Right here right now

I sometimes joke that it is difficult for God to become incarnate in Ireland, because we tend to push him back up into the sky, while we fill the void with saints, relics, and novenas, all supposed to help us get up to God! Poor St Peter seemed to get it wrong more than most of the apostles; in fact, it seems that everytime he opened his mouth, he had to change feet! One of the many times Jesus had to correct him was at the Last Supper, when Jesus took a basin of water and a towel, and knelt at the apostles' feet, and began to wash their feet. Peter was shocked, and refused to allow Jesus to wash his feet, but Jesus told him that, unless he allowed this service be rendered, he could not be one of Jesus' disciples. Here was God, in Jesus Christ, meeting the apostles, not just where they were, but even at ground level, meeting them from the ground up, in total acceptance. When he had finished this extraordinary act of humility and service, he told them that he had given them an example, and this was how they were to treat each other. No wonder someone asked one time if Christianity had died on the cross with Jesus, because we have not seen much of such service since. The Acts of the Apostles says that Jesus came 'to do and to teach'. In other words, he himself did the service, and then he asked his disciples to do the same. He even suggested that his love for them was to be their ideal in loving others.

The cross is the symbol of Christianity. If Jesus had died in any other way, the cross would still be a very suitable symbol. It consists of two beams, one across, and one down. What comes down from God to me, must go sideways to those on either side of me. When forgiveness comes from God, then I must pass forgiveness out to those on either side. The snag is that, if this forgiveness does not go sideways to others, it ceases to come to me. Jesus said, 'If you forgive, you are for-given ... condemn not, and you will not be condemned ... judge not, and you will not be judged ... be merciful, and you will have mercy shown you ... by the same measure with which you give to others, by this same measure will you yourselves receive...' I think that is crystal clear, and needs very little comment from me. It's extraordinary, when I think that so much of this has been put into my own hands, that I have so much say in my own destiny. The ideal of Christianity is to get the balance between the vertical (up and down line), and the horizontal (the line across). In other words, I don't think God wants to hear me tell him that I love him, thank him, praise him, or I'm sorry, unless the people in my life hear it first. I believe it is more important to seek for-giveness from others than from God. Very religious people can have a really vertical religion, when I can spend a lot of my time talking to God, and I'm not talking to my neighbour. That, I believe, is an abomination. Jesus says that if you bring your gift to the altar, to offer it to God, and there you remem-ber that someone is hurting because of you, leave you gift right there, go away, and become reconciled with that other person, and then, and only then, come back to offer your gift to God. Other people, who live on a totally human level, can have a very horizontal form of religion, where it is just you and me, and us, and there is no Higher Power. This can be a human good, and, like everything human, it cannot last, and will die. It is only the balance between the vertical and the horizontal that accurately reflects the message of Jesus.

Supposing I went into a Leaving Certificate class today, and handed each pupil an envelope, with strict instructions not to disclose the contents to anyone else. Each pupil is to open the envelope in private, and to act on the information it contains. When each envelope is opened, it is found to con-

tain all the questions on the examination papers for the following summer. I imagine I would have friends for life!
During the remainder of the school year, a teacher is trying to
whip up some enthusiasm for a poem, or a project in biology,
and the class knows that it will not be part of the final exam
… pity the poor teacher! In the gospel, Jesus gives us a very
clear preview of the General judgement. The questions will
be scandalously materialistic. I will not be asked about
prayer, religious experiences, or church observances. I will be
asked about food, drink, and clothes. Jesus identifies with the
poor so much, that whatever I did for them, he will count as
having been done for him. When I was hungry, thirsty,
naked, a stranger, or in prison, what did you do to help me?
That is the acid test of my Christianity. Before Jesus came, the
prophet said that the Messiah would be recognised when the
blind could see, the lame walk, and the poor would have
good news preached to them. When Jesus did come, John the
Baptist sent some disciples to Jesus to ask him if he really was
the Messiah, and Jesus told them to look around, and judge
for themselves. The blind are beginning to see, the lame have
begun to walk, and the poor are hearing good news being
presented to them. When he sent out his disciples, he told
them that what would prove that their mission was genuine,
was when the blind began to see, the lame began to walk, and
the poor were having good news preached to them. If a man
from Mars arrived among us today, and asked 'Are you
Christians, or do I have to look somewhere else?', what could
we say to him. As someone put it one time, if we were arrested,
and brought down to the local police station, and charged
with being Christian, how many of us would get off scot-free
for lack of evidence?

Studdard Kennedy died in 1929, so his poetry is around
for a while. The following is an excerpt from one of his
poems,

When Jesus came to Golgotha, they hanged him on a tree.
They drove great nails through hands and feet, and
made a Calvary.

They crowned him with a crown of thorns, red were his
wounds, and deep,
'Cause those were crude and cruel days, and human
flesh was cheap.
When Jesus came to Birmingham, they simply passed
him by.
They wouldn't touch a hair of him; they left him there
to die.
'Cause folks had grown more tender now, they
wouldn't cause him pain.
They simply passed on down the road, and left him in
the rain.
Still Jesus cried, 'Forgive them, for they know not what
they do'.
And still it rained a bitter rain, that drenched him
through and through.
All the folks had gone home now, there was no one
there to see,
As Jesus crawled against a wall, and sighed for Calvary.

In a way, I feel that Christianity is on trial in today's world.
Let me put it this way, by using figures from a seminar on
evangelisation in Switzerland a few years ago. Imagine there
are only 100 people on this earth, all in the one village. On
today's facts, 67 of them would be poor, while 33 of them
would be at various levels of being well-off. 93 of them
would have to watch, while 7 of them spent half the money,
have half the bath tubs, and eat one third of the food, while
those 7 would have ten times as many doctors looking after
them as the other 93 put together. That is not the real problem, though, from our point of view. The real problem is
when the 7 have the nerve and the gall to attempt to evange-
lise the 93! They tell them about the beautiful Saviour they
have, who teaches about sharing, feeding the hungry, etc,
while the 7 throw out more food than would feed all of the 93.
They build bigger and better basilicas and cathedrals for this

God of theirs, while the 93 find it increasingly difficult to find a place to live. They transfer monies, and open new and better bank accounts, while the 93 find it more and more difficult to get something to eat. The bottom line must surely be this: If the 7 are so stupid and so blind that they cannot see the frightful contradiction of their situation, then, surely, they cannot expect the 93 to be that stupid, to be that blind!

It is not my intention or desire to lay a guilt trip on anyone. All I am trying to do is to emphasise what I believe the gospel is about. I can rationalise it till the cows come home, but there is no escape, because Jesus has presented us with a programme for living, and it is very simple and direct. I am not going to transform the world, I'm not going to solve its problems, nor am I going to feed its hungry millions. Must less am I going to change the hearts of the other millions who have away more than they need, but will not share. I am answerable to God for myself, and my own conduct. It may simply be a cup of water, or five minutes of my time, but it just has to be about giving. God gives me nothing for myself, and it is a fact of Christianity that it is in giving that we receive. Jesus has arranged things in such a way, that, no matter which way I turn, I bump into him. 'Whatever you do for the least of these, that's what you do for me.' An old monk was praying when Jesus appeared to him, and the monk was in total rapture at the power and beauty of the presence, when the door bell rang, and he knew it was one of the many beggars who came to the monastery door every day. He left to attend to the beggar, and was delighted, on returning to the chapel, that the vision of Jesus was still there for him. He thanked Jesus for staying till he returned, and Jesus told him that, if he had not gone to feed the poor man at the door, he certainly would not have waited for him to return to the chapel.

Jesus came to set up his kingdom among us. His kingdom was on this earth, but not of it. A good way to understand this is to consider the situation of an embassy. It is a building in a country, but it actually belongs to another country, from which an ambassador has come to live. My generation would remember times in the past when a Cardinal in Hungary went into the American Embassy there, so that the communist were not able to arrest him. The same thing happened with some Pentecostals in Moscow. The country in which the embassy is based does not own the building, or the property on which it stands, and has no authority there. That is what the kingdom of God is like on this earth. If I enter it, I am free from the evils of this world, with its false values and wrong priorities. This kingdom is totally opposed to the kingdom of this world, where money, power, pleasure are gods, where the importance of people is determined by their status and wealth, and where it is a case of the survival of the fittest. The values of the kingdom of Jesus are very very different. In that kingdom, Jesus is Lord, and what he says is what matters. In the world, people obey the stock exchange, political opinion polls, tam ratings on television. Jesus said 'If you love me, you will obey me.' Doing what Jesus tells us, is the first rule in his kingdom, and he spoke at great length about feeding the hungry, and caring for the outcast. The second rule in his kingdom is that everybody is important. The most disabled person on earth is here with as much right as the greatest genius that ever lived. The world does not believe this, when it says that people are dispensable, whether through abortion, euthanasia, or heedless, destructive wars. If you live according to the rules of the kingdom of this world, you can get your power from money, political clout, or social standing. If you live in my kingdom, says Jesus, I will supply the power. The kingdom, the power, and the glory are his. To summarise the three rules of his kingdom again … Jesus is Lord; everybody is important, and Jesus supplies the power. My vocation, as a Christian, is to contribute towards the building up of his kingdom on this earth. Jesus asked us to pray to the Father 'Thy kingdom come. Thy will be done on earth, as it is in heaven.'

There was a blacksmith, who lived and worked in a very poor part of the world. One day, an angel came to him to tell him that God wanted him to come to live with him, in his kingdom. The blacksmith explained that the people around him were very poor, and he was the only blacksmith, and, without him, they would have no one to mend their ploughs or shoe their horses. He asked the angel to petition God to leave him among the people for another while. Several years later, the angel returned with the same request, and, this time, the blacksmith explained that a poor farmer had just died, and left a widow, and a young family. He, the blacksmith, had taken it on himself to save their little crop for the family, and to help keep the farm going, until the older children were old enough to run things themselves. He asked the angel to petition the Lord to leave him around for another while. This happened twice more, and, each time the blacksmith was involved with helping someone, and the angel went away. Eventually, the blacksmith grew old, and was tired, and he asked God to send his angel one more time. When the angel appeared, the blacksmith told him that he was too tired to go on, and he would be grateful if God would now allow him to go to live in his kingdom, to which the angel, with a smile, replied, 'You have been living in his kingdom all these years. All that remains now is that you rest from your labours, and enjoy the Lord's company, without the struggles, and the hardship.'

One of the proofs of who Jesus was, was that the blind would begin to see. We know that he is in us, when we begin to see things as they are. When our eyes are opened, and we recognise him in the outcast, the AIDS sufferer, the homeless. Once I have begun to be Christ to others, I will begin to see Christ in others. After the last war, a monastery was being repaired from the damage inflicted by the bombing. The main building was restored, and most of the original structure was back in place. A visitor was puzzled to find a statute of Jesus in the garden, which had not been restored, and which had both arms missing. When he asked about this, he was told that it had been decided to leave the statue the way it was, as a reminder to people that we are now the hands of the Lord, and while we were available to do his work, it was not necessary to do anything with the statue. There is a story told about Puccini, the composer of *Madame Butterfly*. He was writing the score for an opera called *Turandot*, and he felt that, because of age and ill health, he was not going to be able to complete the work. He called his pupils around him, and explained his predicament, and asked them, should he fail to complete the task, that they should accept responsibility for finishing the work. Puccini died before the work was completed. His pupils took what had been written, and studied it at great length. They got a feel for what the composer was about, they captured the spirit of the work, they imbibed the inspiration of the maestro, and they set about finishing the score. At a later date, in the La Scala Opera House in Milan, Toscanini, one of his pupils, conducted the orchestra in the first public performance of the work. It was sheer brilliance, and the audience was being swept along with the power and genius of the work. Suddenly, Toscanini stopped the orchestra, turned to the audience, and announced, 'And it was here that the master died; but his pupils took up his work, and continued it to the end', and he turned to the orchestra, and continued the performance. At the end it was greeted with enthusiastic acclaim, and is reckoned to be one of Puccini's greatest master-pieces. It is said that it is impossible to distinguish where the master stopped, and where his disciples took over. As we say in a prayer in the Mass, 'That we might live no longer for ourselves, but for him, he sent his Holy Spirit, as his first gift to those who believe, to complete his work on earth, and to bring us the fullness of grace.'

Jesus compares his relationship with us to that of a shepherd and his sheep. The parable is clear and simple. It is the day of judgement. The king is on his throne, and he separates the sheep from the goats; the sheep on his right go to eternal life, the goats on his left go to eternal damnation. The element of surprise in the parable is that both the sheep and the goats are utterly astonished to find the degree to which Jesus has identified himself with the poor, the needy, the oppressed. Those on his right have, of course, been feeding the hungry, putting clothes on the poor, and taking care of the sick, but they are completely surprised to hear Jesus say that when they were doing that they were ministering to him. Those on the left are even more surprised to hear Jesus identify himself so completely with the poor and the oppressed. They are shocked; if they had known that Jesus was in need, of course they would have done anything for him. But they hadn't ministered to all those poor, helpless, and sick people, because they were too busy being religious, and pious, and worrying about the letter of the law. What a surprise it was to learn that, in not ministering to them, they had rejected Jesus. Both groups are equally shocked to discover that their eternal destiny is being determined by just a few questions. There are no questions about how often they went to church, what theology they had learned, or how successful they had been in life. These questions are not raised. The questions that determine their destiny are: Did you feed the hungry? Did you care for the sick? Did you visit those who were in prison, or in special need? Lord, make me a channel of your peace. Where there is darkness, let me bring your light. Where there is hatred, let me bring your love. Where there is despair, let me bring your hope, and where there is hunger, let me bring your food. Amen.

11 The firm

I like to think there is some sort of logical progression in these chapters, as we move from considering our Christian calling, to our place within the church, and the place of the church within the plan of Jesus. Let us begin by pretending there is no such thing as church. I read the gospel, and, as I reflect on the message, I wonder if this would really work. This does appear to be a very radical message, one of the most revolutionary proclamations of all time. It speaks about the proud being knocked off their perches, and the humble being raised up. It speaks of food for hungry people, and of God being on the side of the down-trodden and oppressed. It promises much, but I need to find out if it can deliver on those promises. If it can, then nothing on this earth could ever continue to be the same again. I decide to try an experiment. I gather a group of people who are going to help me with the experiment. There are several conditions that must be applied right from the beginning. Firstly, each member of the group must be different from the others. What we hope to do is form a body, and if all were similar, we would end up with all heads, hands, or feet. As I look around my assembled group, it is evident that they meet that first requirement. The second condition is a little more difficult. Each member must accept the fact that all of the others are different, and not expect them to be carbon copies of him or her. Unless this is accepted as fact, the experiment won't work, because the stress will be on uniformity, rather than unity, as if we were in the business of producing Hitler Youth, all goose-steeping out the door together! The third requirement would be that it is accepted as fact that each is uniquely gifted, and, that whatever gifts one possesses are to be made available to the group. In other words, it must be accepted that God gives me nothing for myself. He didn't give me my gift of speech to go around talking to myself! The image I would use would be a mirror, or the engine of a car. I take the mirror, and shatter it. Then I give a piece of the shattered mirror to each one in the group. Each reflects some part of who Christ is, and when we put the pieces back together again, and everyone makes each part available, only then, as a group, do we reflect the face of Christ. I take the engine of a car, and I give some vital part to each member of the group, and we will soon learn that the car cannot function until each makes available to the group the part entrusted to each. There is a very impressive phrase for this, when we speak of unity in diversity. In simple English, this means that, although we are each very different from the other, we can be very united, with a common purpose, without destroying the unique and special qualities that make us different. As human beings, we have so much in common with each other, that it would be a great pity if we allowed the few ways in which we differ to keep us apart. Until we begin to live with this freedom, I cannot see much hope of the Christian churches coming together. If the coming together means that one church swallows up another, or one church saying 'We will have Christian unity, when you all are prepared to give up your beliefs, and become part of us', then I would not wish to see such a travesty, and have it called unity, in Jesus' name.

Jesus came on earth, did what he came to do, and then returned to the Father. He sent the Holy Spirit to complete the work of our salvation, and to guide us safely home. The primary work of the Spirit is to bind, and to unite. The trade mark of Satan is division and conflict, dividing and conquering. The awful destruction and genocide going on, a few years back, in what used be known as Yugoslavia, is a good example of an evil force at work. When people come together, in unity, to work for the good and welfare of others, ... that is the work of God's Spirit. The apostles were very different from each other in many ways. Poor Peter always seemed to get it wrong. Thomas was insecure, and needed constant re-assurance. Philip was not too bright, and needed things spelt out in great detail, while John and James had their mother come to Jesus to put in a good word for them, to ensure they got posts of responsibility in whatever sort of business he was going to set up. Jesus never tried to turn Peter into a James, or John into an Andrew. When the Spirit would come, they would share a common spirit, and that would unite them, as no earthly force ever could.

When the Spirit came upon Mary, it was to avail of her body, of her flesh and blood, to provide a body for Jesus, who would be God incarnate, God in a body, among us. Later, the Spirit came once more on Mary, and the apostles in the Upper Room, and once again, the body of Jesus was formed. When Jesus returned to his Father, he brought the body he had with him. Now, through Mary and the apostles, he would have a new body, and his work would continue, until the last sheaf of wheat was harvested into the store-house of the Lord. This time, the Body of Christ is formed of members that are sepa-rate individuals, all joined and united with the common Spirit of God. The role of the Christian is to contribute to-wards providing the body, and God will provide the Spirit. When Mary asked 'How can this be?', she was told that the Holy Spirit would come upon her, and the power of the Most High would overshadow her. That is exactly what happened at Pentecost, when the church was born. St Paul never met Jesus in person. He was a very religious Pharisee, who was completely committed to destroying the early church, which he saw as a serious menace to his Jewish tradition. He was on one such journey of commitment, when he was thrown from his horse, on the road to Damascus, and a voice asked him, 'Saul, Saul, why do you persecute me?' His name was Saul, which he later changed to Paul. Saul asked, 'Who are you?',

to which the voice replied 'I am Jesus, whom you are perse-
cuting.' From that moment on, Paul thought of Jesus and
church as being one and the same. Jesus had identified himself as being persecuted, when, in practice, it was apostles,
disciples, and followers that were being thrown in jail.

So far, I am speaking about the church in theory, and saying what it is intended to be, and how Jesus thinks of his
church. I am not saying the church you and I know, has always lived up to that ideal. I will now look without fear or
favour on what has happened in practice I have shared something of what I think the church is, or should be, rather than
talking about what the church is not. At this stage, I need to
say that the church is not the bishops and priests, even
though that part of the church has been over-emphasised to
such an extent that one could be excused for making this mistake. We hear it said, in official church circles, that the church
is not a democracy, but is an hierarchical organisation that
will not allow criticism of its teaching. Let me put that in simple English, before commenting on what it says. The church
is not like a political party, where people are elected to office.
Priests and bishops are appointed. The Pope is the only one
who is elected. Personally, I think that is a great pity, especially
in the case of bishops, where the priests and people of the
diocese don't have a say in who should lead them. Religious
Congregations, monasteries, and convents frequently elect
their superiors. I also consider the very word 'superior' as
being a sad choice of word, and, thankfully, it seems to be on
the way out. As someone said one time, anyone who thinks
he's superior has a problem, and anyone thinking he is a
major superior has a major problem! The hierarchical organisation part has to do with a structure of authority, reaching
from the Pope, through the various levels of ordained members, to the laity. Obviously, no matter how many nice words
we use, the laity are at the bottom. I never thought this would
ever change, to be honest with you, but I now believe that we
have begun to see the dismantling of this structure. I believe

much of this structure comes from a misunderstanding of authority, and power. In the language of the world, those words imply having rights over others, and being in a position where others have to look up to those in authority as being some sort of superior beings. Jesus himself said that the world thinks this way, but that must not be the way among his followers. He said that he came to serve, not to be served, and the greatest in his kingdom are those who serve. From the point of view of management, and practical structures that facilitate the on-going mission of the church, I believe in special responsibilities, and I also believe in having competent people involved in the decision-making process. Jesus was not at all haphazard and laid-back to the point where there was no organisation in what he did. He selected a few of his apostles for special occasions, he organised the people in groups before feeding them with loaves and fishes, he sent a few of his friends ahead to prepare for the Last Supper. Nowhere, however, is this seen as delegating power and authority to them. All of this has to do with proper order, and common sense. I don't wish to get bogged down in this whole authority bit, but I do think that bishops and clergy have got to see their place, more as people with a basin of water and towel, ministering to others, rather than being ministered to; in the service of others rather than lording it over anybody. In the following chapter I will share how I see the present fall-off in vocations, and where, I think that will lead the church. All I am dealing with now is that constant barrier one comes up against when we speak about church, and where this is confused with bishops and clergy, to the exclusion of the main, and most important part of the church, the laity. This concept is totally understandable, because of the way things have been up till now. Constantine did nobody a favour when he became a Christian! He was a Roman emperor, and, in a way, he almost took over the show, and made it look more like a secular power. His princes, in their castles, became the example for what came to be called princes of the church, where bishops ended up living in palaces! In our own day, the bishop's residence has usually been called his palace. This was a sad travesty of what Jesus had in mind, and, thankfully, we are beginning to see the end of this. I believe this wrong witness has alienated many people from the church, because, no matter how we try to defend it, it is totally at variance with what Jesus had in mind. I do not think that the church should be above criticism, and, to pretend that all has been well, is a denial of the truth. I am not despondent, or unduly upset by any of this, because I believe that, no matter how far we wander from the ideal, the Spirit will continue to guide the church back into the way of the Lord. It is one of the greatest proofs of the Lord's involvement with the church, that it has survived every possible scandal and corruption in the book. At this very time, indeed, the church seems to be in travail, and we can have reason to hope for the birth of something entirely new. I know that the church will continue to be there when you and I are dead and gone. I would love to live to see a much humbler church, that is not above criticism, and that can be big enough to listen to the diverse voices within it. In fairness, it must be said that no church has ever submitted itself to such open scrutiny, and self-examination as the Catholic Church did at the last Vatican Council. The insights gained then, and the ideals restated then, can actually bring the church back to what Jesus had in mind, when he entrusted us Christians with the message of the gospels. One can just hope and pray that those ideals will be kept in sight, and that the direction clearly pointed to by the Holy Spirit will be faithfully followed. In the meantime, we need great patience, because change on such a large scale, can be all too painfully slow. I live in the hope that the work begun by Vatican II will be brought to completion, like the words of Paul, when he prays, 'May the work begun by the Lord be brought to completion within you'. I don't pretend to have any inside information, but, it did seem to me that quite a lot of effort has been put into slowing down that work, of keeping it under control, and of holding on to a lot of what should have been discarded. Prudence and caution are all very well, but, when they stultify growth, and freeze us into inactivity, they cease to be life-giving. That is why I have to trust God's Spirit to complete the work he has begun, 'until Christ be formed' anew in his church.

Obviously, the church is not a building, made up of bricks and mortar. It is a gathering of people, who share a common spirit, and who have a common view of our role in the world. The central purpose of church is its witness value. When I worked in a parish, I never concerned myself unduly about people who do not attend church. I believe with all my heart that when those who attend church begin to show evidence of the positive effect of that on their lives, that others will want to come along, and be part of that. 'See how these Christians love one another', was the remark of people who witnessed the early church in action. Jesus prayed at the Last Supper that we might be one, because that would be the only acceptable proof that the Father had sent him. He told his disciples that other people would know they were his followers if they loved one another. Witnessing to the gospel is the main purpose of the church's existence.

I remember seeing a notice outside a church in England one time which had, in bold letters C H -- C H. Underneath was the question, 'What is missing? Answer: U R!' I also remember a church gathering being asked to spell the word church, and the emphasis was thus c h U R c h. A minister surprised his congregation one Sunday, by announcing that the church was dead, and there would be a funeral on the following Sunday morning. The following Sunday, many showed up, if only out of curiosity. There was a coffin in the sanctuary, with the lid to one side. The minister invited the congregation to come forward to view the remains. Imagine their surprise, as each looked in the coffin, and saw their own faces reflected in the mirror on the base of the coffin! Yes, in-

deed, we are the church, and it is a test of our maturity that
we are prepared to take our place in the church, warts and all.
I cannot change the church by leaving it. I can react or respond to what I see there. One man told a priest that he
would not go to church, because they were only a bunch of
hypocrites, and he wanted to have nothing to do with them.
The priest smiled, and suggested that maybe he might come
along sometime, because there was always plenty of room for
one more hypocrite! If I look at the vast amount of good that
the church has championed down the years, the care of the
leper and outcast, the homes for the disabled, and the huge
undertakings to feed the hungry of the world; if I look at this
honestly, and without bias, and if I am honest enough to look
at my own contribution, then I may well have to concede that
I cannot point a finger, or throw a stone.

The church has survived every effort to suppress it down
the centuries, by tyrant and dictator. It has been to the fore-
front in standing up to injustice and oppression. The life of
the church is in greatest peril whenever it tends to conform,
and to be used to preserve the status quo. It was thus, for example, in Latin America, but all of that seems to have
changed totally. In that part of the world the church has become the voice of the helpless, and the champion of the
down-trodden. In this way, we can see the church as the salt
of the earth, and as a light to the world. It has had its failures,
and it has lost its way, and even some of its Popes were very
far from what one would expect from the leaders of a
Christian people. And, yet, the church survived, and continues to push ahead with its task of evangelising the world.
Some years ago, missionaries went in their thousands to the
developing and underdeveloped nations. Today, the church
is showing signs of more vibrancy in those parts than anywhere else in the world. Pope John XXIII prayed for a new
Pentecost for the church, and, I believe, that he got one. The
details of this is something I will look at in the following
chapter.

Suffice for now to say that we are living in times of great change, not least, within the church. Change does not come easily to such a large and ancient organisation, with thousands of years of experience behind it. It would be wrong to throw out thousands of years of wisdom, just for the sake of having something new. It is a process of becoming, rather than arriving anywhere. New is not always better, and no matter what comes along, the church has seen it all before. One could summarise all attempts to reform the church as nothing more than trying to get back to the church Jesus founded. As I said earlier, I believe that Pope John got his new Pentecost, and I see many signs that we are living in the Acts of the Apostles of that second Pentecost. I believe we are at the end of an era, and the beginning of a new one. Most of what I have said in this chapter has been about the era that is coming to a close, while the following chapter will look at the era that is now beginning.

12 Watch this space

I believe we are coming into a very exciting, but trying time for the church. The winds of change are blowing, and, I believe the church must listen, and have the courage, and trust in the Spirit, to be willing to be led by the Spirit. I imagine that many a bishop went to Vatican II very happy that all was well with the church, but, as events showed, the Lord didn't think so. In a way, he pulled the mat out from under a lot of what had been, and we still have not put any better alternatives in place, in most instances. For example, it must be obvious that we are coming into the age of the laity in the church. I think the Lord has had enough of a clerically-dominated church, and, it would seem, he is about to give the church back to the people! This will not be easy, for many reasons. Apart from bishops and clergy not wishing to relinquish authority, relatively few people among the laity are trained, prepared, or willing to take up the responsibility that will be theirs in the not-too-distant future. The greatest need in the church, at the moment, is the formation of the laity, and I am not speaking of religious knowledge, or catechism answers here. I speak of information, based on education, leading to formation of Christian community, leading to transformation of the church. We must begin with information, with solid, and down-to-earth religious education, that is gospel-oriented, and that brings people into a personal experience of Jesus Christ. At present, apart from Life in the Spirit Seminars in Charismatic Renewal, there is very little evangelising going on within the church. There may be plenty of lectures, and we can have tapes, books, and videos all over the place, but what we need are people already evangelised, sharing with others who are ready to be evangelised. If I am not involved in evangelising others, it's simply because I myself have not been evangelised. In the context of the two great opening and closing sentences in the gospel, if I have come and seen, I will certainly want to go and tell.

I believe the place of the laity in the church is so central, that God will arrange a total dry-up of vocations to priesthood, if he has to, until this injustice in the church is addressed, and dealt with. I am not at all concerned about vocations to priesthood or Religious Life. I know there is a good reason for what is happening, and I will share some thoughts on that later. For now, however, I just wish to stress that, like it, or lump it, the church is going to be given back to the people. The biggest concern is that we are prepared to do all we can to ensure that people are prepared, and willing to accept their new role in the church. Many generations of being told to 'pay up, pray up, and shut up' can produce a very indifferent, and silent majority. This position is not going to be reversed overnight. Nothing worthwhile will happen if changes are seen as 'concessions' that are grudgingly given; if change comes about because there is absolutely no other way around a problem; or if the institutional church becomes so stubborn and insensitive that it is seen to be irrelevant to the lives of people, anyhow, and they just lose interest. The Holy Spirit has, as always, a central role to play in this, and, often when the Spirit is at work, the solutions are so evidently simple, that intelligent people would never have discovered them, in their search for comprehensive solutions for complicated problems. Genius is the ability to discern the obvious, and the Holy Spirit is expert in this area. From my experience of Retreats, Missions, parent-teacher meetings, etc, I am totally convinced that women form the backbone of the church, and, until they have equal say in church affairs, there will be little progress in the whole area of renewal.

The only realistic way I can grow into the future is to ac-

cept that nothing is ever going to be the same. Spare me the
details of what it was like when you were a kid, and you
walked ten miles in your bare feet to every novena, parish
mission, or Sodality. Those days are gone, and to yearn for
their return is to walk backwards into the future. Life is a
whole series of letting-go's, and that applies as much to
church, as to families. Nothing in life can remain static, because only God is constant, the same yesterday, today, and always. I believe that it is not the world that changes first, and
then people change to adopt to the world. I believe that people are always in the process of change and evolution, and, of
course, every new development in science or technology is
brought about by people, and not the other way around. In
the past, bishops had kingdoms, armies, and all the trappings
of earthly and worldly power, but, thankfully, that would no
longer be tolerated, or practised. As time goes by, we see
things differently, we get a different perspective, and we
grow in our ability to comprehend. No one but God can claim
a monopoly on truth and right thinking. I believe we are getting a humbler church. At Vatican II, members of other
churches were invited to attend, and there was a very edify-
ing witness of mutual acknowledgement, and understanding. Apologies, and requests for forgiveness were exchanged,
for injustices of the past, and there was a respect shown, one
for the other. This was a quantum leap from how things were
in a former age. It is witness like this that sustains my optimism, and enables me hope that we are at the beginning of a
whole new time in the church. In fact, I would go so far as to
say that the work of the Spirit is of such a nature, that his
most effective work is being carried on in secret, unsuspected,
like seeds germinating under ground, and, then, suddenly,
one day, we look and see something wonderful unfolding. In
my heart, I believe we are about to reach such a time in the
history of the church. I was walking in the mountains the
other day. I came across an area where there had been a gorse
fire some months ago. I examined the black remains, and,

yes, here and there I saw shoots of green grass beginning to emerge. That is exactly how I see the church today. My work brings me into contact with much of what is best in Renewal, and that is the source of my optimism.

Religious Life is a charism, or a gift in the church. God does not take away his gifts, once he has given them, and so, Religious Life will continue, but, obviously, in some new form. Religious Life, as we knew it, is finished, as convent after convent closes, and Religious-run schools are being handed over to lay staff. As I travel around the country, I notice the ruins of old monasteries, and I am reminded that this was what was there before Religious Life, as I have known it, began. Most Congregations of Brothers or Sisters I know began within the past two hundred years. Two hundred years from now, there will be something completely different. At present, as Religious Life, as we have known it, is disappearing, there are people experimenting with new ways of living such a commitment. What I am saying is that everything within the church is in a process of continual change, and nothing will ever be the same again. Our choice is one of mission, or maintenance. If we are involved in maintenance, we will surely die, and the sooner the better. If we are involved in mission, we will never die. That promise of Jesus goes with those who do his work his way. Sometimes I detect an air of despondency, when people speak of the fall-off in vocations to Religious Life, as if the whole structure of the church was in jeopardy. This same despondency is far from the hope that must always accompany Christians on their journey, because we are followers of a leader who has overcome the enemy, and who has triumphed over all the forces that would destroy his church, and harm his people. Despair, in any form, has no place in the heart of a Christian. In fact, I believe that the only real sin for a Christian is to lose hope. St Peter has a marvellous sentence in his second letter, where he says that 'You should always have an answer ready to give to those who ask you the reason for the hope that you have.'

Regarding vocations to priesthood within the church, I believe there is need for a new definition of priesthood, an understanding of priesthood, and its place of service in the lives of people. Is it possible that God is deliberately letting the numbers come down, down, down, until the laity is given back their proper place, and that injustice has been redressed? This would not surprise me, and, I am prepared to believe this to be the case. It is not my intention, nor is it within my competence, to review the history of priesthood down the centuries, but, if I did, I could show that priesthood has not always been what we have known it to be. What does the future hold? I do not know, but I certainly am not concerned about it, because I trust Jesus to be there for his people, and I trust the Spirit to inspire, to guide, and to lead. I will be honest, and say that I hope the future will see women priests, and a married clergy, but I will not be so naive as to think that will happen in my life-time. What I do believe, however, is that, whether I am alive or not won't really matter, because I pray only for what the Lord sees as best for his people. Jesus said that he would not leave them as sheep without a shepherd. I must not take this literally, of course, as if the bishops and priests were the only shepherds, and all the laity were sheep. Just as Jesus commissioned Peter to feed his sheep, so, I believe is he commissioning many people, laity included, to take on leadership roles in the church.

And that brings me to ministries in the church, which are being revived after many years of neglect. Let me say very emphatically, right from the beginning, that lay ministers, of any description, are not there to help the priest. No, no, no! These ministries are as much part of the church as sacristans and Mass servers, except they are much more solemn, sacred, and sacrosanct. I think it important that we retain a vision of the ideal, even when we fail to achieve it. Therefore, when I speak of ministries, I speak of the ideal, of how, I believe, they are intended to be. Calling someone up to read at Mass is just not on. Unless the reader has reflected on, studied, prayed about, and become familiar with the spirit of the passage, that person is not qualified to proclaim it. To read it, yes, but God's word must be proclaimed. In the old days, when an invading army was driven back beyond the border, heralds went from town to town, and, in a public place, for all the assembled multitudes, they proclaimed the good news to all and sundry, announcing that the enemy had been defeated, and the country was safe. This was a time of joyous acclamation, and anyone approaching the gathering would be left in no doubt that they were being told good news. I remember reading about an incident in the life of Eamonn Andrews. The local priest asked a young lad to tell Eamonn that he was reading at Mass the following morning. The priest received a letter from Eamonn, saying that he was unwilling to go up there, unprepared, to read the lesson, without having had time to study, to ask about it, and to pray about it. He said that he normally spent a full week preparing a television programme, and proclaiming God's word was much more important than that. With one day's notice, and no copy of the reading in his hands, he regretted that, in conscience, he would not be reading the following day. Would that we had more like him to blast people out of their slip-shod approach, where functional performance rather than ministry is the name of the game. If the importance of the ministry itself is not stressed, we could end up with the reading being played from a tape recording, which would be the ultimate obscenity.

Ministers of eucharist are there in their own right, and, again, I stress, are not there to assist the priest. If John or Mary are ministers of eucharist, and ten priests concelebrate the Mass, nine of the priests should sit in the sanctuary, while John, Mary, and the main celebrant distribute Communion. Treating ministries in any other way is a charade, and a very subtle way of being seen to empower people, while, in fact, we are only using them, when it suits ourselves. At Mass, there are many ministries operating, and the priest is presiding at the celebration, as one among several ministers. To highlight something very important, it would be significant, but not necessary, if the priest left the sanctuary, during the readings, and sat in the pews. This would give correct focus on who exactly is ministering to the community at this particular time. I would emphasise that ministries, as we have them today, is an attempt to return to what was there, before the clerical church assumed all ministries to themselves, and the laity were expected to sit back, and be ministered to, without being actively involved.

As I've said before, nothing will ever be the same, and, I could have said that if I had lived in any century up till now. I speak now, however, of changes in our time. We don't build basilicas or cathedrals anymore. The concept of Christian community is being rediscovered, and I believe the building in which we celebrate eucharist, should also be used for many other meetings of the local community. The more uses the building serves in the up-building of the local community, the more relevance the church will be seen to have in the lives of the people. If people gather there for a Neighbourhood Watch meeting on Monday, for a Residents Association meeting on Wednesday, or a Senior Citizens meeting on Friday, they are more likely to return to join the worshipping community on Sunday. The idea of mission is changing greatly in today's church. Gone are the days when we were into converting people, when we sent missionaries to the most remote tribes of Africa, where we put clothes on the natives, and taught them to become good Europeans, and to get rid of all that held them to their past. Indeed, a few shamrock on St Patrick's Day, and a few bars of 'The night of the Kerry dances' was a very welcome bonus, that brought joy to the heart of the weary missioner! I do not wish to belittle the hard work and dedication of missionaries of the past, but, if they learned to respect the culture they found, and if they themselves were brought on the road of their own conversion, then they were truly blessed. If the concentration was on the need for the natives to change, and become what we had decided they should be, then we were involved in colonialism, and Europeanising. That is not the same as evangelising. In today's world, one would hope that it is the missioner who is first converted, by the adjusting he or she has to make to present a credible face of Christ to those to whom they minister. If the missioner goes through a conversion experience, then the witness of such will constitute a powerful sermon, that will not go unheeded among the people of an area. All I am saying here is that missionary endeavour, like every other aspect of church activities, is going through fundamental and basic transformation.

The church in which I grew up was not unlike the seamless robe of Jesus that the soldiers cast dice to win. The church was seamless in that it was all of one piece, as far as I was concerned, where we all marched to the beat of the same drum, and we were a vast silent majority. Everybody in my part of the country went to Mass on Sundays, to devotions during Lent, or to the annual parish mission. There was a uniformity there that was totally predictable, and deviation from the norm was not to be considered. In fact, I do remember the shocked whispers about certain locals who emigrated, and rumour had it that they were a disgrace to their mothers, and to their church of origin, by not continuing to be faithful to the rigid moral code, and strict church observances they had received in their local national school. Without wishing to be simplistic, it would appear that we were not much better than our environment. A lot of our religion was deeply effected by the social milieu in which we lived, rather than coming from some deep sense of conviction. When at home, I did as others did, and when away from home, I fitted in with whatever was the norm. I would suggest that we are developing a much healthier church today. The church is no longer a large uniform gathering, where all think and act alike, but is becoming smaller groups of much more committed people.

In the gospel, as Jesus spoke to his disciples, some of them turned and walked away, because they did not like what he was saying. Jesus let them go, and he turned to challenge the others, to make sure that their staying was the result of a decision, and not inaction. A group of Christians had gathered in Russia some years ago, and were holding a prayer meeting, when the door was broken down by the boot of a soldier, carrying a huge gun. He stood in front of the gathering and said, 'If any of you don't really believe in Christ, get out now, while you have a chance'. Several made for the door. The soldier then closed the door, came back in front of those who remained, smiled, and said, 'Actually, I believe in him, too, and I believe we are better off without those!' It is quality not quantity that the church requires today. The time has come to stop catechising people in our schools and sacramentalising them in our churches, when no one had thought of evangelising them. This way, we were engaged in producing vast hordes of spiritual illiterates.

I have heard the question asked 'Who needs Church?' My answer is that I do, and that my church needs me. With all its faults, it reflects exactly what's within us all, and is no better or worse than we ourselves are. I think it is important that I use a critical eye when I look at the church, or I will settle for mediocrity and aimless conformity. The one thing I have said again and again throughout this chapter is that nothing is the same anymore, that the whole thing is a-changing. Let me finish with a story that, I think, summaries the big difference between the church of my youth, and the church of today. A chicken and a pig were out for a walk. The pig wasn't too bright, and tended to repeat the ideas of others. 'They are very good people down in that farm-house' said the chicken. 'They are, indeed', agreed the pig, 'they are very good people.' 'They are very good to us,' said the chicken. 'Yes, indeed', said the pig, 'they are very good to us.' 'Do you know what I was thinking?' said the chicken. 'No', said the pig, 'what were you thinking?' 'I was thinking we should do something for them.' 'A very good idea', said the pig, 'I think we should do something for them. What did you have in mind?' 'I was thinking', said the chicken, 'that we should give them something.' 'A very good idea', said the pig, 'I think we should give them something. What did you have in mind?' 'I was thinking', said the chicken, 'we should give them bacon and eggs.' The pig stopped in his tracks. 'No way', he said. 'For you that's only a little inconvenience, but for me it's a total commitment.' And that, my friends, is the big difference between the church of yesterday, and the church that is now evolving. The men of violence, the war mongers, the drug pushers, the pornography peddlars are all totally committed to what they are about. If I am not part of the solution, I also am part of the problem. Half-hearted, lukewarm, indifference is more destructive than direct assault. Jesus says that if we are not for him, we are against him. There is no in-between. It's not a question of a little inconvenience anymore. Anything less than total commitment to Jesus and to his message is unworthy of our Christian calling.

13 Remembering

In the following two chapters, I will share some thoughts that I find useful in helping understand the Mass, and its place in the life of a community. I will also discuss some of the difficulties that people have shared with me over the years, and see how we can deal with those. I don't at all pretend that I have all the answers, but I consider the subject important enough to give it my best shot. Firstly, let's have a quick look at where the Mass came from, as we know it. I am using the word 'Mass' now, even though I may use the word eucharist later on, or eucharistic celebration at another juncture. These are just different names for the same thing. Anyhow, to go back into the origins of the Mass, we have to go back to the time of Moses. Sacrifices, or offerings made to God have always been part of what people did from the beginning of time. This applied equally whether the offering was made to a pagan god, to many gods, or to the God of Israel. Moses was bringing the people back through the desert into the promised land. In one way, we could say that they believed in one God, and, then again, they were just as liable to make a god out of brass, and adore that. On one occasion, when Moses returned from speaking to God on the top of the mountain, he discovered that they had made themselves a golden calf, and were adoring that. Anyhow, God made an offer to them, through Moses. God said that he would be their God, if they would be his people. He was offering an agreement, and they were asked to consider it, before making a decision. The big word for this sort of agreement is covenant, because, like a marriage, which is very serious, it is

more than just a contract. I go into a shop, I give the lady a
certain amount of money, and she gives me a newspaper.
That's a contract; we owe each other nothing, the job is over
and done with. If a couple getting married entered a contract,
rather than a covenant, they would find themselves taking
turns washing the dishes every second meal, and each would
be responsible for cleaning one half the house. Very soon this
would become ridiculous, and would be based on law, and
not on love. And so, God offered a covenant. A contract can
be broken, whenever I choose, but a covenant is lasting, even
when I am unfaithful to it, and it can, and must always be renewed. God said that if the people accepted his offer, they
would have to change their behaviour in several ways, not
least that there must only be one God from now on. In fact, to
give them definite guide-lines, God offered Moses the Ten
Commandments, so that, in keeping these, the people would
be living within what God expected from them. Again, if they
accepted this, God suggested that this covenant should be
solemnly celebrated with a meal, at which the covenant
would be renewed, and everyone would be reminded of the
offer that God had made.

Throughout the centuries, the Hebrews had this solemn
annual meal, during which the words of the covenant were
read, and agreed to, and they celebrated their special relationship with God. It was at such an annual gathering that
Jesus announced the greatest good news of all time. In effect,
he said that God was offering a new, and never-ending or
eternal covenant, when he would be our Father, if we agreed
to be his children. If we accepted that, he was offering two
rules, or commandments, and by keeping these, we would
behave as he wished, where the emphasis was on loving
God, and loving neighbour, and seeing one of those as every
bit as important as the other. If we accepted that offer, he
would give us a meal, during which we could renew our
commitment to this new covenant, while reminding ourselves of the details. Part of this meal, which Jesus celebrated

with his apostles, was the fact that he gave them a wonderful teaching about God's plan, his own love for them, and what would happen when the Spirit came. He then took a basin of water and a towel, got on his knees at their feet, and began to wash their feet. This was all part of the attitude that would go with this new and eternal covenant. It was by their love for each other that people would know they were his disciples. It was by their unity that people would know that he had come from God, because division and conflict are the trademarks of Satan. It was an empowering awesome meeting of a humble, loving, and serving God with a pitiful, immature, and uncertain group of people, who would soon deny him, betray him, or desert him. He had offered them a covenant, however, rather than a contract, and this could always be renewed. Jesus knew the human heart, and he had personally experienced many human weaknesses, as he lived in our mortal flesh for the previous thirty-three years. If I may digress for a while, and say that I think it was a pity to have made the connection between Confession and Communion that was part of what I experienced, growing up. There was great stress on making sure that I was good enough, worthy enough, before I dared approach the altar for Holy Communion. I believe in reverence, of course, but the idea that I could make myself worthy, or good enough, is a carry-over from the times of the Pharisees. I think it is a pity that eucharist, or Holy Communion, has never been seen as potentially just as forgiving an encounter between Jesus and the sinner, as Confession, or the sacrament of reconciliation. Naturally, I still see a need for sacramental reconciliation with God, but I also believe that opening my heart, like the publican at the back of the temple, and asking Jesus to come in there as my personal saviour, and bring a whip of cords, if needed; I believe that to be a powerful moment of reconciliation. The strict puritanical teaching of former times, kept people away from Communion for the slightest failing, and that, I think, was a failure to understand and appreciate the vast scope of love and acceptance being offered us in this new and eternal covenant, that Jesus unveiled at the Last Supper.

Meals have always had a special ritual meaning in our lives. Nowadays, this has gone away beyond the wedding breakfast, or the silver jubilee celebration. Families go for meals now on First Communion and Confirmation days. They spend hours over a meal, returning from a funeral, where many memories are exchanged of the loved one, who has just passed away. I meet an old friend, after many years, and we agree to meet for a meal, so that we can celebrate the memories together. Meals have taken on a whole new ritual-istic importance in our lives today. Of course, we must admit that these rituals could be total charades, and be totally insin-cere and superficial. It's like everything else we do, when the level of sincerity and genuineness is determined by the spirit that inspires the action. Because of the necessity for balance between the two commandments about loving God and neighbour, Jesus warns us that coming to the altar is not something we should take lightly. He says that if I bring my gift to the altar, and there I remember that someone is hurting because of me, I should leave my gift right there, go away, be-come reconciled with that person, and then return to offer my gift. Once again, I stress that there is nothing automatic about God, nor is there any magic formula for a quick-fix, without doing things his way. I could well have more to answer be-fore the judgement seat of God for the Masses that I attended than the ones I missed. It might be common enough to hear-ing 'missing Mass' being listed as a sin, while seldom hearing that attending Mass, when such was a meaningless charade, was also a sin.

Christianity is about a group of people who come together to provide the hands, feet, voice, and, indeed, body, so that, through them Jesus can continue his work on earth. These people form the body of Christ, and it is important to remem-ber that Jesus is most present among such a group. In other words, Jesus is present in Communion, but he is more pre-

sent, if I could put it that way, among the worshipping community. In the community, he can touch, and be touched, he
can speak, and minister, as well as be ministered to. He can be
hurt, rejected, or ejected. I remember saying Mass one time
for a gathering of people, and in the middle of the homily,
this poor woman, the town drunk, came up the middle of the
church, talking to herself. She climbed in over everybody,
and took her place in the front seat. She began to interrupt
some of my words of wisdom, and the eyes of everyone in the
church were on her, and if looks could kill, she would have
died on the spot. Thankfully, no one attempted to remove her,
and she fell asleep. I myself was holding my breath, hoping
that she might be accepted as she was, because if I ever come
across the body of Christ without the wounds, I know it is a
phoney. And here was one of the wounds, and it would have
been very wrong to be so religious and pious, that such as she
would not feel welcome among us. Do you see what I mean
by the wonderful way in which Jesus has put us all on the
spot!

As a Christian community, our principal assembly point is
around the altar, because we are a eucharistic people, above
and beyond everything else. It is there that we are most challenged to become what we are called to. It is there that any
lack of sincerity or genuineness in our Christian commitment
is most evident. Jesus chose bread and wine as his way of
being present among us, as food and drink. He could have
chosen any of a thousand other ways, but this was the one he
saw as having most meaning. The grains of wheat are gathered, and, after a process, are converted into a single unit,
bread. The grapes are gathered, and, again, after a process,
are converted into a unit, wine. A group of people assemble,
and once again, after a process, are converted into a unit,
community. Now we crushed the wheat and the grapes as
part of the process, but how do we form community?
Certainly, not by crushing! Imagine, if you can, that I stand
up on a table, and begin to speak to an assembled gathering.

My voice is low, and is not carrying to the folks at a distance, so they gather closer to me, in their efforts to hear what I am saying. As this happens, they may become aware that, the closer they come to me, the closer they have come to each other. As they gather around me, they notice that they are touching each other. That is how community is formed. By coming closer to Jesus as individuals, we discover that we also come closer to each other. Imagine that I inflate a large balloon. I use a black marker, with which I put one large mark, and many smaller marks here and there around the outside of the balloon. I then let the air out of the balloon very slowly, and, as I do so, I notice that, as the balloon contracts, the smaller marks all come closer and closer to the larger one, and, in doing so, are coming closer to each other.

The central purpose of eucharist is to give honour to God, and to build up the community present. It is all about community. I heard of a lady who was very involved in a lively worshipping community. One weekend, she was down the country, where she attended Mass. The whole thing was so boring, and uninspiring, and even the priest looked thoroughly bored. She could hold back no longer, and she prayed out loud, 'Praise the Lord!', upon which the priest came down to her, told her this was the House of God, and 'we don't praise the Lord here'! How perfectly, but, pathetically true! That is why it was such a distortion, when I was a boy, and the priest stood with his back to me, muttering in a language I did not understand! I remember writing an article some years ago, asking the question 'Are there too many Masses in Ireland?', and I concluded that a Mass that does not build up the community present, would be better omitted, because, again, I stress, that there is nothing automatic about this, and it is wrong to think that a Mass is a Mass, whether there is any community present, or whether the community present is involved or not. I would strongly contend that the Mass is not a private spiritual exercise for the priest, or for anyone else. If I am confined to bed, taking part in a Mass on television or on the radio can help to put me in touch with God, but is but a temporary substitute for being part of the worshipping community, and being actively involved in what is going on. Carrying things to a ridiculous extreme, what do you think of having Mass on a video, that I can play when I feel like doing something religious?!

Jesus bowed his head on Calvary, and said 'Yes' to the Father. He said he had come to do the Father's will. He died once, and once only. I heard a woman giving out about people leaving Mass before it ended, and she said, 'Did they ever go to school, did they ever learn their catechism? Surely they know that poor Jesus dies at the Mass, and you'd think they'd wait till he's dead!' No, Jesus does not die at the Mass. His death on Calvary, his 'Yes' to the Father, like any other 'yes', can be repeated again and again. The prayer of Jesus on Calvary can be offered to the Father, but, unless it involves our 'yes' to Jesus, then we are not part of it. At Baptism, we had water poured on us, as a symbol of our willingness to die. Water represented death for the Hebrews, and they had to pass through the waters of the Red Sea to enter the Promised Land. In baptism, I am committed to do my dying during my life, through the millions of little dyings that are part and parcel of Christian living … through forgiving, sharing, caring, listening, assisting. I bring the water of my baptism back to church, drop by drop, and as the priest holds up the chalice, with the wine in it, which represents the death of Jesus, he puts a drop of water into the wine, to represent our contribution to the offering. Once again, I can be caught in a total charade and mockery, if those dyings are not a reality in my life. Being present at Mass is powerfully challenging, and it presupposes a maturity that may not always be present. At this stage, I must say that Christianity, from the very beginning, was for adults, and that can account for the fact that young people often cannot see the richness of meaning and symbol that is part of its rituals and rites.

There are two parts to the Mass, the liturgy of the word,

and the liturgy of eucharist. The word liturgy, loosely translated, means a particular work, that has an underlying meaning. It is an external task, that gets its richness from the depth
of meaning this is behind the action. If I am being welcomed
to a function by a rabbi in Jerusalem, I could very well be offered a pinch of salt to take. This is a symbol of my sharing in
the bitterness of their exiles, and the struggles of their people
throughout history. In the first part of the Mass, we are nourished with the word of God. On Sundays and special feasts,
there usually is one reading from the earlier part of the Bible,
called the Old Testament, one from one of the Letters of St
Paul, or one of the other writers, and finally, a reading from
one of the gospels. There is an infinity of difference between
the words in a Bible, and something I might read from the
daily papers. The word of God is inspired by the Spirit of
God, and has within it, the power and presence of God. As
the centurion said to Jesus, 'Say but the word, and my servant
will be healed', or as Peter said to Jesus 'At your word, I will
let down the net.' The priest then usually gives some teaching
based on the readings. Without wishing to comment on the
ability of the priest to give a teaching, I must say that the ministry of teaching played a major part in Jesus' dealings with
his apostles. We can use words like sermon, homily, preaching, or any word we wish, but, in the final analysis, it is about
teaching, and applying the message to my daily life. The
Mass is a meal, where God invites us to share a meal with
him, to sit at table with him, and share in the life of his own
Son. The word of God is part of the meal, because, as Jesus
said 'Not on bread alone do people live, but on every word
that proceeds from the mouth of God.' We are nourished by
his word. In the early Christian church, when the people
gathered to celebrate eucharist, which they called the breaking of the bread, it was always preceded by what was called
the breaking of the word. The word of God was also thought
of as food, … food for the soul, the mind, and the spirit. Then
there is the liturgy of eucharist, which, roughly, has three

parts, all linked to each other. Firstly we offer the gifts, God accepts and transforms them, and offers them back to us. This is the Offertory, the Consecration, and the Communion. In the early church, those who were not yet baptised, and fully enrolled members of the community, were allowed attend the liturgy of the word, but had to leave before the liturgy of eucharist. Each had a special significance, and the people were very aware of this.

It is important that we have some understanding of what we do, and why we do it. Worship of God is as old as the human race, and ritual offerings have always been part of that worship. The main difference between Mass and any other form of worship that preceded it, is that Jesus himself is offered to the Father, and the community present is called to be of one mind and one heart in offering the sacrifice. This is both privilege and responsibility, and I cannot have one without the other. Over the centuries God has made himself present to his people in many different ways. He spoke to his prophets in the whispering wind, he spoke out of a burning bush, and he came among us as one of ourselves, in the form of a helpless baby. Jesus said that where three or more were gathered in his name, he would be there in the midst of them. In eucharist, he makes himself present to us in the form of food and drink. When the Israelites wandered through the desert for forty years, God provided food for them, in the form of bread, called manna, which they gathered each morning. It was life-giving, and sustaining. Moses, at God's instructions, struck a rock, and water gushed forth, to quench the thirst of his people. God was seen by the Israelites as someone who was always caring for them. For us, his presence in eucharist is a constant presence, reminding us of his continual concern for our well-being.

In summary, then, we have a constant reminder of his new covenant with us, and our obligation to continually re-commit ourselves to our side of that offer. God is faithful, and he never reneges on his promises. Through the prophet, he told us 'I will never forget you, my people. I have carved you on the palm of my hand. I will never forget you, I will not leave you orphan, I will never forget my own. Should a mother forget her baby, or a woman the child of her womb? Yet even if they forget, I will never forget my own.' At the Last Supper, when the first Mass was celebrated, Jesus said that we are his friends. He was condemned by the religious leaders of his day, because he was a friend of sinners and outcasts, and he even ate with them. Eucharist is where the sinner is invited by the Saviour to join him in a meal, as a special friend, and to cement that friendship in the breaking of bread. The Indian tribes passed around a pipe of peace, as a symbol of acceptance among the tribe. Jesus shares his own life with us, and greater love than this no person can have.

14 Celebrating

In this chapter, I hope to be as practical as I possibly can, and, hopefully more helpful in ensuring that we understand the place the Mass plays in the life of the Christian community. It is important to remember that, just as no person is an island, but is part of the mainland, so no one is a Christian apart from the Christian community. The Spirit of God is offered to the community, rather than to the individual, and it is only to the extent that I am attached to the community, and draw my life from there, that God's Spirit can effect the good in me. Jesus used the example of the vine and its branches, and unless we, as branches, are attached to the vine, we cannot have access to the source of life. As I said in the previous chapter, Christianity is intended for adults, and in the early church, those who joined the Christian community were mature adults, who had plenty of experience of life, with all its struggles and pit-falls. It is difficult for the young, who have been protected, and who have not yet come to grips with the many tensions of life, it is difficult for them to have enough maturity to admit to failure, brokenness, and powerlessness. It is difficult to speak seriously about life to anyone under 35 years of age! Part of being young is a feeling of self-sufficiency, and a desire for independence from the restraints of home, school, and even God. The Prodigal Son left home, full of confidence in his own ability to survive, and to overcome. It was only when he had hit skid row, that he took stock of his situation, and came to his senses. A teacher I had one time used tell us that experience is a very good school, but the fees are often very high. I would defend the right of youth to learn from

their own mistakes, just as many of us adults learned important lessons. However, I would argue that maturity is not always a matter of age, as I have come across some young people who show a marvellous level of maturity, and I have
come across some adults who seem to be very immature.
When I hear young people say that 'I get nothing out of
Mass', I smile, because I believe they do not see the full impli-
cation of what they are saying. Doing things just because I get
something out of it is not always a good thing, obviously, and
could lead to very selfish behaviour. Poor granny will get no
more visits from me, if I continue to get nothing out of her for
visiting her! I'm saying this with tongue in cheek, of course,
but it might be no harm to give it a thought.

I am most open to a Higher Power when I come to experience my own powerlessness. The eucharist is a power-house,
where my spirit is recharged. Right at the beginning, we remind ourselves that we are sinners. We confess that fact, and
ask for forgiveness. If that reminder sinks in, and I go out the
door with a desire to seek forgiveness, or to grant forgiveness, then my presence there has been worthwhile. The acid
test of Mass in my life is what happens when I go back out the
door, at the end. I remember, one time, as I watched people
leaving Mass before it was over, I went to the microphone,
and with a straight face, I said a prayer for the faithful departed!
I was trying to make a point, and I believe I did, because the
exodus did not take place the following Sunday. At the end of
Mass, we get a blessing, and are sent out the door 'to love and
serve the Lord, and each other'. In other words, the real
power of eucharist begins after I go back out the door. A couple kneel in front of me to get married, and each makes all
sorts of lovely promises to the other. That is totally meaningless, unless, after going out the door, they give meaning and
life to those promises for the rest of their lives. What happens
after they leave the church gives meaning to what happened
in the church. Similarly, I baptise a baby, and we all hope that
twenty or thirty years from now, this adult of the future will

give meaning to the words we now say on his or her behalf. Otherwise, we are wasting our time. I do not believe that sacraments work automatically, of themselves, right there, independently of other elements in our lives. Going to the sacrament of reconciliation does not obtain forgiveness of sin, if there is unforgiveness in my heart for another, or if I have no intention of making an effort to get it right. Going to Mass places a responsibility upon my shoulders. Personally, I would love if we were invited to sit down for a few minutes at the beginning of Mass to reflect on what we are about, and if there is anyone out there hurting because of us. Then, before we leave, to sit down for another few minutes, to reflect on what must happen now, when we go out the door, and how we can carry Jesus to those we meet today. In scripture, Jesus says 'I stand at the door and knock. If anyone open the door, I will come in, and will make my home with that person.' I sometimes think that, later on that same day, I hear a knock on the door, and when I ask Jesus what he wants now, he tells me that he wants out again ... out again in my words and actions, to touch the hearts of those I meet, so that I can be his touch-person in their lives. As I go out the door, I can become a channel of his peace, love, hope, and light.

I often joke about what I call the transforming power of holy water! I see people entering the church grounds and the car park. They wave or shout across to each other, and they seem quite friendly. However, as soon as some of them put their fingers in the holy water font at the door, all life seems to leave them, and they look towards the altar with a lifeless stare, and when they are invited to give a sign of peace, they extend a hand that feels more like the tail of a fish! Once again, I am saying this with tongue in cheek, because most people continue to be friendly, and continue to look alive, even after passing by the holy water font! I also smile when I hear people proclaim, after the Consecration 'Lord, by your cross and resurrection, you have set us free. You are the Saviour of the world.' The reason I smile is that some of them don't look too free! I keep stressing that, if I'm saved, I have a responsibility to look saved, otherwise my witness value to Jesus is nil.

There is one custom or expectation that can accompany our Masses that, quite frankly, irritates me. As I offer the Mass I often have a piece of paper on the altar in front of me, with the name of the person for whom this Mass is being offered. This name is mentioned publicly at the beginning, and at least one more time in the course of the Mass. There could be serious trouble, if I decided to include someone else in this same Mass! We say that the sacrifice of Jesus is infinite, but try telling that to the family who are here for this anniversary! This Mass is for one intention, and for one intention only! I heard of a woman who had twin boys, and they were delicate. The weather was beautiful, and the doctor suggested that an hour in the sun each day would do them a great deal of good. Nothing was too good for her babies, so at midday, she put one little lad out in the front garden. She brought him indoors at one o'clock, and put the other little lad out until two o'clock. She did not put both out at the same time, because she wanted each to get the full benefit of the sun, to have the sun all to himself! This is surely ridiculous, but not nearly as ridiculous as someone insisting that a relative or friend is to get the full benefit of this Mass, and it cannot be shared with another.

The most important part of the Mass, believe it or not, is the great Amen at the end of the eucharistic prayer, just before the Our Father. We have had an offering, a consecration, prayers for the living and the dead, and for the church at large. The priest then holds up the host and chalice, and says that all of this is made possible by Jesus, and that all glory and honour belong to the Father because of what Jesus has done. It is then that we proclaim, with one voice AMEN, as if to say right-on, OK, we agree. When we thus have proclaimed Jesus' role in making all of this possible, we can stand up, and together call God Father, and, with a sign of peace, we call each other brother and sister. Now we are ready to share in the meal. In most cases, our method of sharing is far from ideal, but, I believe that change is on the way. What a wonderful thing if the bread looked like bread, and, like the early church, we broke from it, and then passed it to the next person. This way, we are seen to share Christ with each other. Then, by receiving from the chalice, we are seen to drink from the same cup, another powerful symbol of Christian unity. This is part of the big barrier that blocks a crossing of boundaries in common reception of Communion with other Christian churches, because there is a divergence of beliefs in exactly what is meant by receiving Communion, and, it is argued without union, there can be no Communion, which literally means a common union. Please God, some day, and the sooner the better.

I remember having a group of young adults in a secondary school on retreat. I spent a full day offering one Mass. In the morning we reflected on, and discussed our sinfulness, and our need for reconciliation. Some of the pupils felt a need to go to the staff-room to apologise to a teacher for behaviour unbecoming. Others acknowledged the fact that they were being really unfair towards parents or other family members. This part took up most of the morning. We broke for coffee, and from then till lunch-time, we had liturgy of the word. We read several passages, which were discussed, and reflected on. Many of them wrote out insights gleaned from the readings, and these were shared. It was an experience of great power, as the Spirit was evidently active among them. After lunch, we began with an Offertory procession, and the variety of gifts, and the many explanations for the choice of gift, was really inspiring. The bread had been made during a domestic economy class in the school, and the wine was supplied by a teacher who was expert at wine-making. The celebration continued all afternoon. The following day was also very powerful, as we began by sharing how we brought yesterday's Mass back out the door with us, as we left, and what we had

done since, because of being present at the celebration. I myself have celebrated eucharist by a lake-side, on the bank of a
river, and even on the very top of the Cliffs of Moher. All of
those times were attempts to stir up reflection, and to move
the celebration out of the normal cosmetic atmosphere of a
church. Of course, the location doesn't make the celebration
any greater, even if it helps heighten the involvement, or the
attention. All I am saying here is that it can help to understand eucharist better if I think of it as something that involves people, and the place or time or conditions are purely
secondary.

Many of the changes effected in recent years are but an attempt to return to the way things were. When I was a boy, the
priest stood at the altar, with his back to me. This was because
God was away out there, somewhere. Then we remembered
that Jesus said he would be found in the midst of us, so we
turned the altar around, and the priest and people faced each
other. There was nothing more profound or theological about
the change than that simple reason. In former times, before
several priests could concelebrate the one Mass, our larger
churches had many small altars around the sides, and several
Masses would be going on at the one time. This caused some
pious souls to move from altar to altar, receiving Communion
at each, without actually attending a full Mass at any one.
This caused a rule to be introduced, limiting Communion to
once a day. Now, with the abuse being corrected, people may
receive more than once in the same day. What I'm saying here
is that these changes are just intended to return to what was
there before abuses made it necessary to introduce some new
rule. For example, people always received Communion in
the hand, until, in evil times, some people brought the host
home with them for black masses, or for ritual desecration.
This lead to the introduction of a rule confining reception of
Communion to the tongue, when the priest stood over the
person until the host was consumed. Again, now that the
abuse has been removed, so can the rule, and so we can again

receive on the out-stretched hand, if we so choose. These changes, including the return to the native language from the universal use of Latin, are nothing more than enlightened common sense. Change is slow and tedious, and it can be hindered when people have not been given a reason why the change is being introduced. For example, if a minister of eucharist is seen as just someone helping the priest, then those who never settle for second best, will walk all around the church to receive Communion from the priest! This expression of immaturity might be avoided, if someone took time out to explain what is behind the change. Mass is so central to our lives, that there is need for on-going education, to ensure a deepening appreciation and understanding.

No matter which way I turn in matters of the Spirit, sacraments, church, or community, I always end back with Jesus Christ. If I have accepted the fact of Incarnation, that God actually has come to walk among us, then nothing can ever be the same again. I believe that Jesus wants to be part of all we do, and everything we undertake. This applies equally to our worship of God, and our building up of community. He makes himself available to us, so that in gathering around him, and coming closer to him, we may come closer to each other. It is absolutely necessary that I have an openness to knowing Jesus Christ, that I open the door, and he will certainly enter my life. There is a story told about the classic painting of Jesus standing at a door, and his right hand is raised to knock on the door. When the painter first put this on display, his attention was drawn to an obvious mistake he had made,....there was no handle on the door. The artist explained that this was not a mistake, because the door is the door of the human heart, and there is only one handle, and that is on the inside.

Jesus in the gospel was Saviour, he was in search of sinners, and anyone who was lost in any way. He compared himself to the good shepherd, who would leave ninety-nine sheep to go searching for one that is lost. Among those who were in touch with their brokenness, their blindness, their powerlessness, Jesus found people who were willing to listen, and to accept what he offered. This is the normal way to meet Jesus. When I am aware of my limitations, my fears, my mortality, I become more open to the fact that I, too, need a saviour. Not much point in speaking about a saviour to someone who is most certainly in control of everything, and has no feeling of being lost in any way. I believe that, as life goes on, I come more and more in touch with my humanity, and with my helplessness. It is like as if my little boat is gradually drifting out of the harbour,...out into the deep. I can experience fear, anxiety, and occasional panic. It is at such times that Jesus is closest, hoping that I turn to him. I look at people in church at a funeral, and I often think how much they need this Mass, more than the person who has died. I have celebrated a Mass for healing on Friday nights for some years now, and, when I see a young mother coming in the door with her baby, or a man being helped along who is obviously wasting with cancer, I am confirmed in my conviction about the truth of what Jesus said 'Only those who are sick need a doctor'. If I am honest, I will have to admit that being a member of the church is like going into a hospital where everybody is sick, including the matron! We all are in great need of the healing touch of Jesus. 'Lord, I am not worthy to receive you; say but the word, and I shall be healed.' Notice that I said a Mass for healing, not a healing Mass, because every Mass is a healing Mass. What happens there depends on the hearts of the people present. I learned to talk by talking, to swim by getting in the water, and to love and appreciate the Mass by being present. I do not pretend that this is easy, because sometimes the presiding priest can be anything but inspiring. However, while not excusing such, I believe that I must not look outside myself for excuses for doing things, because most of the reasons are within, and the other person is just giving me an excuse for doing what I really wanted to do, anyhow. In many ways, yes, the Mass can be boring. It can be boring because it is not intended to be entertaining, and I am the one who may need stimulation and excitement to get me involved in something. Once again, I may have to look within my own heart. I admit that the presiding priest can have a strong influence for inspiration or desperation, and I agree with people who find that they have to travel to a church in some other area, to feel nourished, or to experience a sense of community. I myself have made a habit, over the years, of attending Mass in various churches, just on speck, where I was able to mingle with the crowd a few rows from the back. I would have to admit that several of those celebrations were anything but inspiring, and I wouldn't be in any great rush to return. Obviously, this didn't stop me going to Mass, no more than a bad experience with my local doctor would cause me to have nothing more to do with the medical profession. Anyhow, as I finish this chapter, I hope I have given you food for thought, some useful insights, and, above all, a greater understanding and appreciation of the greatest prayer at our disposal.

15 Listen, Lord

There is a big difference between praying and saying prayers. I could teach a parrot to say a prayer, but I could never teach a parrot to pray. I can speak words, but the spirit in the words determines how helpful or hurtful they are. It is the spirit in the words that reaches the listener. Someone could be devastated with a terrible tragedy, and I just don't know what to say. It really doesn't matter what I say, if there is real love and concern in my words. On the other hand, I could say all the correct words, and be very careful in my choice of words, but, if they are not inspired by love, they will not be helpful. Praying is a very wide field, and there are endless ways and means to pray. One of the ways is by using words. The words used, however, have to have God's Spirit in them if they are to become prayer. It is important, right from the beginning, to emphasise this vital principle: it is the Holy Spirit who turns my words into prayer. In the movie 'The Ruling Class', this man is in a psychiatric hospital, and his problem is that he thinks he's God. One day, to humour him, the psychiatrist asked him how he discovered he was God, and he replied, 'The way I discovered I was God was that I was praying and praying for years and years, and then, one day, I woke up, and discovered I was only talking to myself.' Saying prayers, without the Holy Spirit being involved, is simply talking to myself, and I shouldn't be surprised when nothing happens, and I don't even feel inspired myself. Now, like Jesus, there is one simple problem when it comes to the Holy Spirit. He will not be involved in anything unless he is asked! So, right from the start, let me make this point perfectly clear: when I begin to pray, I should simply ask the Holy Spirit to be in my words, to turn my words into prayer. That's all. It's as simple as that. Try it, and see what happens in your prayer.

The second thing I want to emphasise is that the organ God gave me with which to pray is the heart, not the tongue. In the main basilica in Assisi, up over the main altar are the words *Si cor non orat, in vanum lingua laborat*, which, in simple English, means if the heart is not praying, the tongue is wasting its time. It is a very long journey from the head to the heart. I could have enough intelligence up in my head to write a book about God, while, down in my heart, I might not really believe in God. 'Head people' can be dangerous, because they can be full of brilliant theories, and bright ideas, but, down in their hearts, they could be moral cowards, or totally paranoid. If I want to really make contact with God, and, therefore, pray, I must go downstairs into my heart. 'These people honour me with their lips, but their hearts are far from me', is how God described the Israelites one time. Those words could apply to all of us, at some time or other, I'm sure. I mentioned, earlier, that, without involving the Holy Spirit, I am only mumbling words. Jesus compared the Holy Spirit to a fountain of living water that rises up from within a person. In other words, the Spirit comes up from the heart. 'From the abundance of the heart the mouth speaks', says Jesus. Once again, I need to know what kind of spirit is in my heart. If it is a spirit of greed, of anger, or of jealousy, that is what will inspire my words and actions. The thing I must remember is that the Spirit of God is always in my heart, even if ignored, or not availed of. I received God's Spirit at my baptism, and his presence in me was confirmed at Confirmation. The problem usually is that I have the Spirit, but the Spirit may not have me. I can very well get on with my life, living and acting independently of the Spirit. That is why I said earlier that, if I want to pray, I must begin by getting in touch with the Holy Spirit, and involving him in the exercise. St Paul goes so far as to say that we do not know how to pray, but the Spirit of God can give meaning to our words, and can speak within us in ways that are not possible with words. I pick up a telephone to make a phone call. Suppose the line is broken, and I do not know that, I will soon discover that my efforts at making the call are not being very successful. In fact, I will discover, sooner or later, that I just cannot make the call. If the Spirit is not involved in my attempts to pray, then the wire is broken, and I cannot make connection. When Jesus did what he came to do, he returned to the Father. He sent his Spirit to complete his work. In other words, nothing of God gets done around here anymore, without the Holy Spirit being directly involved. To use the language of the business world, the Holy Spirit is the Executive Member of the Trinity!

A man returned to his car in the car park of a supermarket, to discover that the side had been badly dented. His shock was relieved somewhat, when he noticed that there was a piece of paper under one of the wipers. He opened the paper, and read what was written. 'I have just hit into the side of your car, as I was pulling away. The people who witnessed this are still watching me. They think that I am writing my name and address on this piece of paper, but they are wrong.' Prayer is much more than simply going through the motions. Jesus said the Pharisees believed that, by using many words, they would get God's attention, but there is much more to prayer than that. When I was a lad, we were told that prayer was a raising of the mind and heart to God, to adore him, to praise him, to thank him for his benefits, and to implore his grace and mercy. It is very difficult to define prayer, as if it were some sort of action that is clearly marked by a beginning and an end, and that produces a certain result. Vocal prayer is speaking to God, and, like any conversation, its value lies not in the length, but in the depth. It is not so much me raising myself, or any part of me to God, but going downstairs into my heart, and getting in touch with God there. Once again, I cannot think of this outside the central truth of Incarnation, where God has come to where I am. The genuine charismatic becomes a contemplative, because the closer I come to God, the less reason I have to shout! I will speak about charismatic prayer later on. For now, suffice it to say that it involves giving free rein to the Spirit within, while singing, praying, or listening, as the Spirit leads me. Prayer is one name for working on my relationship with God. Like any other relationship, there is a personal dimension to it. I am speaking here, of course, of my own personal private prayer, as distinct from community worship, such as being present at Mass. Like any other relationship, it grows through honesty and truth, and dies as a result of insincerity, and sham. I come before God, exactly as I am, exactly as he sees me, without any pretence, or desire to impress or deceive. Jesus speaks of the Pharisee who went to the temple to pray. It was important to him that he should be seen by others, because he took pride in his goodness, and his religious observance. The Pharisee stood up, and prayed out loud, for all to hear. He told God how good he was, and he listed off all the good things he had done. God was to be silent, and listen, because the Pharisee was speaking! This was a complete reversal of roles, because real prayer is not so much me talking to God who doesn't hear, as God speaking to me, who may not listen. Jesus told the story to teach a lesson about prayer, and about the attitude we should have when we come before God. The other person in the temple was a publican, a sinner, who dared not even raise his eyes, but struck his breast, and prayed 'Oh God, be merciful to me, a sinner.' Jesus said that it was the publican who went away at peace with God, because he was the one who was honest, and who knew his place before God.

Jesus could have used many different words to describe the Holy Spirit, but he chose the words 'Spirit of Truth'. This was to serve as an antidote to the spirit of lies, who had led the human race astray in the first place. If the Spirit is to be involved in my prayer, then my prayer must be based on truth. God knows what is in my heart, but he respects my right to keep that to myself, or to trust his love and acceptance enough, to share that with him. We all find ourselves in situations where we know what is bothering a friend, and we encourage that friend to talk about it. Hopefully, we will have enough respect and cop-on to back off, and let the other decide just how much is going to be shared. Jesus did not go around the roads of Galilee healing anyone. No, he went around with the power to heal, and the people on the roadside made up their own minds. There were many who died of leprosy, or with blindness, even though Jesus walked right in front of them. Even when some of them did stop him, he asked them what they wanted. It was obvious that one man was blind, and that others had leprosy, but, still they had to ask him. 'Lord, that I may see ... Lord, if you will, you can make me clean.' On occasions, he even asked them if they believed he could heal them, and when they said they did, he told them that it was their faith in him that made them well. In other words, he gave the power to them, and the decision was theirs.

Prayer becomes so much easier when I am honest with God. That includes the times when I am angry with him for something that has happened. Not much point in trying to speak sweet words of piety, when, inside, I am really angry, terrified, or depressed. God sees what's in the heart, and, as the writer of the Psalms says, he knows me through and through; he knew me in my mother's womb; he can read every thought, feeling, and emotion within me. A young lad says, sometime in October, that he wants a bike for Christmas. He never mentions the word 'bike' again. I'm not sure his parents should buy him a bike. If he really wanted a bike, they would be left in no doubt. It is the same with prayer. God always answers sincere prayer, even if it is not the answer we had expected. A young lad had been praying for a bike, and he didn't get one. His pal was jeering him, and spoke about God not answering his prayer. The lad said that, of course, God had answered his prayer, and the answer was

'no'! If God were cruel and sadistic, he would give us everything we ask for, and have a good laugh, because we must
surely ask for things that are not for our good.

In the following chapter, I will suggest practical ways that
may help, when we pray, but there is no one technique that is
better than another. Three priests sat around discussing
methods of prayer. One was very emphatic that the only way
to pray was on our knees. The other disagreed, because he
practised an eastern method, where he sat on the floor, with
his back upright, and both hands held open on his lap. The
third was equally emphatic that the correct way to pray was
to pray as Jesus did, when he cast his eyes up to heaven. The
argument went back and forth for some time. There was an
electrician doing a job in the corner of the room, and he approached them sheepishly to say, 'far be from me to debate
methods of prayers with three priests. But I'll tell you one
thing I have found out about prayer. The best prayer I ever
prayed was one time when I hung by one leg from an electric
pole, in a thunder storm, when the ladder slipped. And you
know something, God heard me!' God is really interested
only in what is in the heart. It is not possible for a human
being to fall on his knees, cry out to God, and not be heard.

Prayer is, above all, giving God time and space in my life.
The length of time is not what matters, because, I believe if I
begin at all to give God time, that I will be lead along into
some further time, when I begin to get in touch with my own
needs. If I'm honest, I must admit that I can always find time
for the things I really want to do. For myself, I love watching
football on television, and I often find myself arranging work
in such a way, to ensure that I will be free to watch the match.
It doesn't always work out that way, but it is never because of
lack of intention and effort on my part. I said earlier that
prayer is working on my relationship with God. Building a
relationship with another requires spending time with that
person. It involves sharing and listening, and part of the sharing includes common interests. If I visit with someone only

when I want a favour, and if I continue to talk about myself only, to the exclusion to the interests of the other, I will not be building a healthy two-way relationship. The greatest contribution I can make to peace in the world is to look in my own heart, listen to the inner voice of conscience, and take whatever steps are necessary to establish peace there. Peace is what I experience when my relationships are the way they ought to be. I must always watch out for selfishness in prayer, because selfishness is most destructive when it is disguised as a good. When I have peace in my own heart, I can contribute positively to peace in the world, by praying for that. Jean Vanier, one of God's special people in today's world, says that some of the greatest movements for good in the world have been brought about by the quiet prayers of totally unknown people. Taking responsibility for my own part in today's world is a sign of maturity, and making my own contribution towards the betterment of the world around me is to develop a generous spirit, and a giving attitude.

The ordinary basic rules of good manners apply in prayer, even more than anywhere else. Jesus was deeply hurt when only one of the ten lepers he healed returned to thank him. Having a grateful heart is something wonderful, and a source of on-going blessing in my life. It is not possible to be grateful and unhappy at the same time. King Lear lamented that 'how sharper than a serpent's tooth it is to have a thankless child.' Ask any parent, and this will be confirmed for you. My relationship with God is deeply effected by how I relate to other people. If I have the honesty to admit to wrong-doing, and to seek forgiveness from another, I will do the same with God. In fact, one without the other is meaningless. St John says that 'if you say you love God, and do not love your brother and sister, you are a liar, and the truth is not in you. How can you say that you love God, whom you cannot see, and not love your brother and sister whom you can see?' Not praying, or not making an effort to pray, is often a sign of something more serious than just not praying. It indicates an attitude that is very unhealthy, and certainly not life-giving.

Service to others is at the very heart of Christian living, and, quite often, praying for another may be the only service I can provide. The most I can do for another is to heal sometimes, to help often, and to care always. I may not be able to heal or to help in a particular situation, but I can certainly pray. Such prayer of service is very pleasing to God, and, as Jesus said, whatever I do for others, he will consider as a service rendered to him. God weighs my prayers, rather than counts them. He criticised the Pharisees for thinking that multiplying prayers made them more effective. His own prayer-life was obviously very important to him, as he continually slipped away by himself, to be alone with his Father. Yet his prayer was also very simple. His apostles asked him to teach them to pray, because, obviously, they were deeply impressed by watching him at prayer. He taught them the 'Our Father', which is a very simple prayer. It is a very down-to-earth prayer in that, after the opening praise to God, all the rest of the prayer is about life among us down here. He gives praise to God, he prays for what God wants to happen among us; he asks just for what is needed today, and he asks God's on-going protection among the evils that surround us. Even when he taught them to ask for forgiveness, this was to be measured by the degree of forgiveness they extended to others. Once again, the balance between the vertical and the horizontal, between God and me, and me and others, must be kept in mind.

Quite often, my most powerful and effective prayers do not require words. I go downstairs into my heart, I open the door, and invite the Lord in. As often as not, prayer is what he does, when I allow him. Prayer has much more to do with attitude than with actions. I have often seen someone sitting by the bedside of a loved one, who is dying, simply holding a hand, and saying nothing. At other times, I have watched as a mother nursed a sleeping baby. There are no words involved, but there is a deep conscious awareness of the other. In the final analysis, it is about love, and when that is part of a rela-

tionship, the words become less and less important. Even
when a mother is speaking to a baby, the words sound like
meaningless gibberish, but there is a relationship there, of
which both baby and mother are conscious. If I came up behind the mother, and heard her say 'Vouchsafe, I beseech
thee, humbly to grant onto me one night's sleep', I would
have good reason to be concerned about the relationship!
Quite often, words can be the weakest form of communication. At a grave-side, a hug, or putting an arm around the
shoulder of another, can be more meaningful than trying to
think of some suitable and appropriate words.

In the following chapter I will deal with listening in
prayer, with what God may have to say to me, if I am prepared to listen. There are as many methods of prayer as there
are people. If we differ even right down to a finger print, and
if we accept the fact that God created each of us to reflect
some special aspect of himself, then don't be surprised that
our relationship with him should be different, and our ways
of being in touch with each other should be uniquely personal
to us. That is why, in speaking of prayer, that I have deliberately kept my reflections on the level of general observations,
rather than being very specific, black and white all the way. I
have to respect God's way of being in touch with you, and
your own openness to respond. The one thing that I say, very
emphatically, is that I must give prayer a definite place in my
life, no matter how great or how small that may be. If I do not
eat food, my body will soon let me know, and the people
around me will soon become aware of that. Food provides
energy for my body, as petrol does to an engine. If I do not
pray, that inner me, that real-self me, will tell me, and very
soon, I will begin to become spiritually malnourished, and
those around me will know that all is not well with me. It
may sound strange, and even arrogant, but I certainly recognise people who pray. I know it in everything they do and
say. There is a health about them that is evident, and they
have a richness of spirit that exudes life to those they meet. A

very popular book on prayer from some time back is called 'Prayer is a hunger'. I believe there is a spiritual hunger within us. We may try to take care of it through material or emotional food, but that emptiness will persist, and that empty place within will continue to cry out for nourishment. As St Augustine said 'You have made us for yourself, O God, and our hearts can never be at rest until they rest in you'.

16 Speak, Lord

While wanting to avoid getting too technical, I hope to share some ways of praying that you may find helpful. Remember that prayer is really what God is doing when I give him time and space. I remember training swimmers years ago, and there was one young lad there, and I was convinced he had what it takes to beat the best. It was very frustrating, because he was so involved in other sports that it was almost impossible to get him to come to the swimming pool. I eventually had to give up on him, and it will never be known what he might have achieved

Let us look at one insight into prayer, for a few moments. I knew a young doctor, who was married with two young children, and they were the centre of his life. Imagine the shock when he discovered that he had cancer, and he was not going to get better. This caused him great anguish, but, when he finally came to grips with it, he took some practical steps to meet the situation. He had visualised himself spending a lot of time with his children, as they grew up, and he had every intention of being there for them as they struggled with their adolescent and teenage years. He would be there when they moved into their independent and interdependent years. Now, he realised that this was not going to happen, so he decided to do the next best thing. He got a tape-recorder, and he filled a c-90 tape with everything he wanted to say to them, in the hope that, after his death, they might listen to this from time to time, and it would help to guide them. It was extremely touching. It was obvious he was speaking from his heart, and that he meant every word he said. What he had to

say was practical, and very reassuring. He told them that he
would always be there for them, that he would always look
after them, and that he had every confidence they would
grow into mature responsible adults. That was several years
ago, and those children are now in their late teens and early
twenties. I know, for a fact, that they do listen to the tape on a
regular basis, and it has been a steady guiding hand for them,
as they grew up. I also confidently expect that they will continue to cherish that message for the remainder of their lives.
They consider themselves fortunate indeed, to have had this
constant reminder, and assurance, and they continue to get
great motivation and inspiration from it. I mention this, because, in many ways, it reminds me of Jesus, and the message
he left with us, the night before he died. In St John's gospel,
chapters 13 to 17, we have the equivalent of that c-90 tape the
young doctor made for his children. Jesus would be killed the
following day, so he spent several hours with his apostles,
during which he gave a message for them, and for all of us,
for all time. He said he would always be there for us, that he
would continue to look after us, and that we would never be
alone. He prayed that we might take seriously what he had
said to us, and that we might live up to all his hopes for us.
He promised that his Spirit would never leave us, and he assured us that his Father loved us as much as he loved Jesus
himself. He gave advice about love, and he spoke of the
marks that would show that we belong to him. I honestly believe that, if, like the children and the tape, we were to read
these chapters from time to time, we would really come to
know and understand the mind of Jesus. That would be a
powerful help when we come before him in prayer. The
gospel is now, and I am every person in it. I have my own evil
spirits, my own form of blindness, my own hungers. By reading a short passage from the gospels, and reflecting on it for a
while, I will be amazed at how my relationship with Jesus
will deepen. One of the big advantages of this is that my
prayer becomes a response to something Jesus says or does.

In other words, he has the initiative, and my role is more that of responding to him, than running the show myself. I would strongly recommend that you get yourself a copy of the gospels, if not the whole Bible. There are little pocket editions available, and I know people who read a little, without drawing attention to themselves, as they get into bed at night, take a coffee break at work, or sit in a parked car. It takes but a few minutes, and it is a habit that is so easy to develop, but it is one that produces powerful results. I remember, some years ago, there was a great interest among the young in the teaching of Chairman Mao-Tse-tung of China. In some circles, those times, it was the 'in' thing to carry Mao's Little Red Book in a pocket, and to read it at bus stops, in doctor's waiting rooms, or anywhere there were a few idle moments. You see, what I'm speaking about is not necessarily something that everyone does, or is generally accepted and expected. Prayer is too important to have fixed and definite ways, without scope for how the inner Spirit might prompt you. There can be wonderful freedom in prayer, just as people with a romantic soul can discover endless ways of telling another that he/she is important to them. I think it important that I dare to be different, if I am to grow into any kind of spiritual freedom.

Mount Palomar is down in southern California, and there is a huge telescope on top of the mountain. It is known that if a photo-sensitive plate is put in the scope, and the lens are opened to outer space for ten seconds, and the negative is then printed, there will be at least ten bodies from outer space in the photo. If another photo-sensitive plate is used, and the lens are left open for ten hours, there will be thousands of bodies from outer space in the photo. I think of prayer as something like that. The more I am open to the Lord, the more of his light will I reflect. Another image for prayer is to look at the beach as the tides comes in. The beach is me, and the tide is the Lord. The tide is the actor, the prime mover, and the beach gets acted on. The incoming tide will make a profound change, as the beach will be smoothed, and cleaned, as all the loose rubbish gets caught up in the water. The beach will certainly change, but it is the tide that causes the change. If the beach resisted change, it would have to jump up and down, and form a wall of resistance to the incoming tide. Real prayer can be risky, because I may hear something I don't want to hear. Jesus came to comfort the afflicted, but he also came to afflict the comfortable! It is, therefore, rightly said that the better form of prayer is when I stop talking, and listen to God speaking.

Just as some people are endless talkers, and they bring that with them when they come to pray, so others are, by nature, good listeners, and they have a great gift for listening. They help more people by simply listening to them, than many of the others with all the talking. Who is speaking, and who is listening is very important in prayer. If I switch on the radio here beside me, I am sure that there are many people talking, singing, entertaining, but I'm certainly not listening. God is always saying something, if I take time out to listen. He, of course, is always ready and willing to listen, should I wish to share some worry or problem with him.

The human heart can actually become a prayer room, an Upper Room, if I choose to allow this happen. Mary, Jesus' mother and mine, is more than willing to take up residence there, so that Incarnation can happen all over again in me, and that, in turn will lead to Pentecost for me. That is why I should always ensure that I get in touch with my heart, right at the beginning of prayer. God's Spirit is in my heart, and, like Mary, Jesus is being formed within me. One of the images I find useful, when at prayer, is to try to enter into the thinking and feeling of a mother, who is pregnant, and who is deeply happy about that fact. As she sits quietly on her own, she gets in touch with what is happening within her. She is very conscious of a new life developing there, and she responds to every stirring of that new life. That's a good image for prayer, where I can go downstairs, get in touch with a new life stirring there, and, all the while, I need only say 'Yes, Lord … Yes, Lord'. Like Mary, I am saying 'Yes', so that the Spirit can work in me, and through me. In this kind of prayer, rather than doing anything myself, I am keeping in touch with what God is doing, and I am giving my whole-hearted consent to that work. Another image is that of a deep deep well, with bubbling living water down in the depths. The well, unfortunately, is filled with junk, old car wrecks, and garbage. I go downstairs, get in touch with this, and I hope and pray that the water, which is the Spirit of God, may rise to the top, lifting all the rubbish to the surface, and dumping it over the side. This, again, is the proper work of the Spirit, and my role is to give permission, to allow this happen. Prayer here is but another example of me looking on, contemplating God at work, and saying my 'yes' to that. When I was growing up, I knew that my parents loved me. I wasn't very good at showing appreciation, because it is so easy to take such love for granted. God loves me, and, when I spend time with him, when I give him time and space in my day, it helps a lot if I am conscious of being loved. The saint is not the person who loves God, but the one who is totally convinced of being loved by God. Prayer is a special way of receiving and returning that love. On a sunny day, I go into the back garden, and sit in the sun; I sit in a deck chair, stay where I am, and the heat of the sun reaches me. If I get a sun-tan, that is what the sun does, when I show up, and make myself available.

Another image that can help in prayer is to go downstairs into my heart, and use my imagination to see what is going on there. I can imagine a house, with dry rot in the walls, and the timber of the windows. There is a large rubbish skip, and the walls are being stripped back to the brick, and all the damaged cement and timber is dumped into the skip, ready to be disposed of. The walls are going to be freshly plastered, and the timber is being replaced. This is an image of the Spirit at work, clearing away the wreckage of the past, and renew-

ing my own inner self. 'I make all things new', says the Lord.
God removes what is not healthy, and he strengthens what is
weak. He touches the areas in need of healing, and he renews
my inner spirit. In Zen Buddhism, for example, prayer involves sitting still, and letting the muddy waters settle within, and, when that has happened, becoming aware of a pearl
of beauty and great price that is there, but was not visible in
the muddy water. In Christian thinking, that pearl is the Holy
Spirit, and when I am quiet, and let the muddy waters settle, I
can be much more conscious of that inner richness. There is
another image, from my early childhood, that I find helpful. I
remember the days I spent making turf in the bog. As the
men dug out the turf, it sometimes happened that a log was
uncovered, which had lain there for many years. This timber
would be very tough, and very seasoned, and, if placed in an
open fire-place, would burn for hours. I sometimes imagine
the surface cracking open, and many logs being raised to the
surface. These represent the hurts, the memories, and the
fears that are buried in my subconscious, under the floor-
boards of my heart, as it were. As they are brought to the surface, the hurts and the memories are healed, and I can get rid
of them. All of these images help us to be conscious of a constant activity going on in our inner spirit, and, in prayer, we
get in touch with that, and become aware of it. Jesus was constantly inviting his apostles to come aside for a while, far
from the pushing crowds, to spend some quiet time with
him. Those were times of prayer for them, and they can be for
us, when we choose to go aside, and spend some time with
him.

In an earlier chapter, I made a clear distinction between
being religious, and being spiritual. This difference is most
evident in prayer. Religion could be called a spirituality of
addition, where I pile on more and more prayers, and hope
that they will lift me out of the quicksand of my own selfishness, and, eventually get me into heaven. This is human endeavour at its most evident. Spirituality, on the other hand, is

a spirituality of subtraction, where I do less and less, and the Lord is free to do more and more. I am not suggesting that I do nothing, like the man whose beard went on fire, and he prayed it might rain! Of course, I do something, like going aside, like taking time out, like calling into a church. What I am saying is that the results that come from that is what God does. I just keep showing up, and will not stop until the miracle happens. And it will happen, as God begins to do things for me beyond my wildest dreams, and things begin to happen that I myself could never effect, by myself. Let us look again at the story Jesus told about the two men who went up to the temple to pray. One delivered a long monologue on how good he was, and how much better than others he was, while the other just fell on his knees, and asked God to forgive his sins. One was preoccupied with what he was doing for God, while the other was asking God to do something for him. One day Jesus visited the house of Martha and Mary. Martha was busy in the kitchen, preparing a meal, while Mary sat at Jesus' feet, listening to him. Martha was annoyed, and asked Jesus to tell Mary come and help in the kitchen. Jesus defended Mary, and said she had chosen the better part. Now Martha was a good person, and someone had to prepare the meal. The mistake Martha made was that she began with what she was doing, and, if she had time later on, she probably would have come out to spend time listening to Jesus. On the other hand, Mary, having listened to what Jesus had to say, and having spent time with him, would probably have gone into the kitchen and prepared the meal then. Again, it is a question of beginning with myself, or beginning with God.

I have already said that there is a vast difference between praying and saying prayers. I hope I have stressed that difference enough by now. Saying prayers can be boring and uninspiring, and I can easily get fed up, and abandon all attempts. One of the special blessings of recent years has been the growth of prayer groups. This is a gathering of people who come together once a week, for an hour or more. During that time, their prayer can vary from singing, to reading the Bible, to sharing some experience or insight, usually finishing with prayers of petition for intentions presented at the meeting. Periods of silent reflection form an important part of each meeting, and, quite often, there is a cup of tea available afterwards, when they can continue to share and enjoy each other's company. There is a community dimension to this kind of prayer that is very life-giving.

This is not a book of prayers, but I would like to conclude this chapter with an outline of a simple guided meditation, something you might like to try sometime. First a quiet place, where you are not going to be interrupted. Sit in a comfortable chair ... close your eyes ... take your time ... make sure you are relaxed and comfortable ... take a moment or two to get ready. If I go out after a shower of rain, I notice a pool of water in one place, and other areas are quite dry. People are like that. Try to be relaxed so that God's love can soak right into the core of your being. Become conscious of your breathing ... in ... out ... in ... out ... OK...now, imagine going down into yourself with one of those breaths, and stay down there. Look around. You are on a beach ... a beach that stretches for miles ... fine white sand ... gentle waves coming almost as far as your feet. Take your time to get into the scene. Look up into the sky, notice the seagulls ... squat down and fill your hand with the fine sand, and let it run through your fingers ... Stand up again, and look down along the beach ... there are people walking towards you ... Keep them in sight ... notice how they seem to grow in height as they approach. They are about fifty yards away now ... something's begun to happen ... The main group have dropped back, and only one is walking towards you ... It is a man ... deep tanned skin ... trimmed beard ... long flowing hair ... Yes, it is the Lord.... It is Jesus ... and he is walking directly towards you. Just remain as you are, where you are ... let him approach you. You see his face now, and the one thing that strikes you is the

smile ... a bright warm glowing smile ... He is almost in front
of you now, and then he stops, and holds out a hand ...
'Come to me ... I will give you rest ... I have loved you with
an everlasting love ... I have carved you on the palm of my
hand ... fear not, be not afraid ... I am with you ... I will never
leave you...' Jesus invites you to walk along the beach with
him ... on over towards the nearby rocks, where he sits
down, and invites you to sit beside him. He looks you
straight in the eye, and says 'I am always delighted to meet
you, and to spend time with you. Even when you forget, or
have no time for me, that's OK, I understand, because I know
your heart, and I know that you are good. I will never ever
condemn you, or reject you, even when you are very hard on
yourself. I will always be there for you, when you turn away
from the pressures, and come aside. I don't ask you to make
any promises to me, but I would be truly happy if you believed my promises to you. That's all I ask for, is that you
trust me, that you believe me, ... because when you do that
you are showing that you know I love you...and that's what
matters. I came to love you, and all I ask is that you accept my
love, and, through me, you will come to know my Father's
love ... and we will give you the Spirit who will be with you
always ... always ... through every situation, even to the end
of time.'

17 Enough's enough

In this chapter, I have decided to write about hope, and I do so very deliberately. There are so many pressures in today's world, that it is becoming more and more difficult to hold your head, when all about you are losing theirs. In a way, life is getting faster, and, like the stunt-man with the motor-bike, riding the wall of fire, I have to move at a certain speed, or I'll come crashing down. We may joke about keeping up with the Jones's, but, I believe that, in our hearts, there is a real fear of being left behind, of being passed out, of becoming an also-ran.

I remember an experiment we used carry out in the science-room many years ago, and, before the sophistication of today, it was really exciting then. A petrol can was used, and through a process, the air was extracted from it, and we watched with delight as the sides caved in. Nature detests a vacuum, and once there was a vacuum created in the can, the air on the outside simply pushed in the sides, to fill up the vacuumed space. Something like that can happen with us, when there is an emptiness inside. There is an open space, as it were, in the heart of every human being, and only God can fill that. We are created in that way, it is part of the maker's design. We can try to fill that space in any way we wish, but it simply will not work. Alcohol, drugs, sex, money, power … all have been tried, and, eventually, were discovered to be false gods, that did not live up to the promises they seemed to offer. The ultimate disaster of all of this, sometimes, is suicide, which, unfortunately, and understandably, has been enormously on the increase, in recent years. Now, let me say something about suicide, before we go any further. It is not my intention, or my right, to judge someone who commits suicide. I have no idea what goes on in a human mind, before making such a decision, and carrying it out. Nor do I know anything about brain-storms, or the types of depression that can cause the future to look so black that anything is preferable to having to face it; or what happens when life goes into a tail-spin, and gets out of control. The reason I make this clarification is, that, while I need to speak about suicide, I do not wish to pass judgement, in any way, on some poor soul who may have taken this option.

Powerlessness is part of being human, in so far as life is not something I can manage, or fix, like a tape-recorder that mangles a tape. If I know anything about the workings of a tape-recorder, I can open it up, free the tape, clean the heads, and have it going again, without any trouble. Life is not as simple as that. The first time I was carried into a church, to be baptised, I was not consulted, nor was I involved in the decision in any way. The next time I am carried into a church, for my funeral, I will not be consulted either, nor will I have any part in the decision-making that will accompany that, unless, of course, I have specified all of that beforehand. To try to run the show in-between is not possible. I own nothing. One heart-attack, or an accident, and it's all over. Trying to play God is insanity run wild, and it always brings its own heartbreak. A young American Indian boy had reached his teens, and was being tested, before admission into full manhood in the tribe. He was brought into the middle of a jungle, and told to spend a night there on his own. The night was long, very long, and he thought morning would never come. His heart beat faster with every sound, with every movement in the under-growth. Several times he thought of running for it, but had no idea where one could run within the confines of a jungle. He thought morning was never going to come. Finally, the dawn began to break, and light began to filter through the trees. As his eyes became accustomed to the emergence of daylight, he began to look around him, to take in the view of what was to be seen. Suddenly, he saw a shadow behind a tree, and, as he approached, he discovered that his father was standing there, and had been on guard there all through the night. He breathed a deep sigh of relief, and immediately thought that if he had known his father was there, he would have slept soundly all night! When I die, and go to heaven, I will discover that my Father was watching over me night and day all my life. If I express any surprise at this, Jesus could say 'But I told you that. I told you that your heavenly Father would take care of your every need, and that he is always looking after you.' No wonder Jesus said that the sin of this world is unbelief in him. He made very specific and detailed promises, and he hopes that we might begin to take those promises seriously. It is the firm intention of Jesus that, once he has come into our lives, nothing would ever be the same again. There was a cave in the deepest part of a mountain, and it had never seen light. One day the sun invited it to come up and visit it, so that it could have an experience of light. The cave was thrilled when it saw light for the first time; in fact, so grateful that it invited the sun to come visit it the next day, because the sun had never seen darkness. The following day the sun came down, and entered the cave, looked around, in surprise, and asked 'Where's the darkness?' When Jesus comes into our lives, he comes as the light of the world, and he says that they who follow him do not walk in darkness, but have the light of life.

Hope is about God coming to write on crooked lines. On a human level, the fall was a disaster, and Calvary was the end of the road, and yet both events were turned around completely, and became occasions of eternal blessings for God's people. It is one of the most remarkable things about the Israelites in the first part of the Bible. No matter how bad things were, they were full of hope that God was with them, and that the Messiah would come, the one who would lead them into freedom. It is one of the tragedies of history, of course, that the Israelites thought with an earthly mind-set, and the only kind of freedom they could think of was freedom from their enemies, from the Egyptians, from the Romans, or from whatever or whoever the oppressor was. When Jesus came to set them free, they tried to make him a king, so he could lead an army into battle. They failed to understand that the greatest enslavement takes place within the human heart. A recovering alcoholic in AA, knows more about enslavement and being freed from slavery than the Israelites ever did. Through experience of our own brokenness and powerlessness, we can come to really appreciate freedom, if we choose to let God be God, and watch him do for us what we ourselves could never do. God doesn't take away the struggles, but he guarantees the result, and the outcome, because, just as he came to the apostles, walking on the water, he comes to us in the struggles. The first and surest way for me to come to know Jesus personally, is when I call out to him in the midst of struggle. The widow of Naim was in the depths of hurts and helplessness, when Jesus came along, and, again, it was like the sun entering the cave, and dispelling the darkness.

There were two boys one time, and one was a pessimist, the other was an optimist. One would find something wrong in heaven; he could never appreciate what he had, because he was always conscious of what he did not have. The optimist was full of hope, and, even if his team was beaten by ten goals, he was quite hopeful they would win next time out. Anyhow, the pessimist was put into a room full of toys, and the optimist was put in a room filled with manure from the farmyard. After an hour, they were checked on. The pessimist was sitting in the middle of all the toys, and he was crying. When asked why he was crying, he replied that he was crying because there was no drum! When the door of the optimist's room was opened, he wasn't aware of that, because he was really busy with a small shovel, and he was shovelling the manure from one corner of the room to the other. He was interrupted, and asked what he was doing, and he replied, with his eyes filled with excitement, 'With all this manure, there's just got to be a pony here somewhere!' And that, my friends, is the difference between hope and despair. Of course, we have to struggle, to shovel, and to work hard, but Jesus guarantees the results. That is an extraordinary aspect of the Christian faith. As I attend a funeral, and see the tears of genuine anguish, I would be present at a school for despair if that was the end of it all. However, as Christians, we believe that it certainly is not the end, and the very best is yet to come.

One of the dimensions of life is that nothing ever remains the same. Everything is in a state of constant change. We are growing older by the minute. All the cosmetic surgery, and wrinkle-smoothing face-cream cannot stop the advance of time. In a way, I seem to just succeed in making ends meet, when something happens and moves the ends. Only God is constant, the same yesterday, today, and always. Any kind of stability in my life is bound up with my relationship with God. Without God, I am like a weather-cock on top of a church, that is constantly at the mercy of the wind, and has no control over which way it points. This is a very stressful way to live, and there is a constant lack of ease, or dis-ease in my spirit. Jesus told us he came that we might have life, and have it to the full. He offers us his peace, and his joy, which, he said would be pressed down and flowing over. I repeat again and again that Jesus gives me nothing, while offering me everything. It is totally up to me whether I am open to his gifts. Sometimes I have to be totally broken before I am prepared to open my heart fully to him. When I'm on the broad of my back, there is only one way to look, and that's up! It is generally accepted that there are no atheists in a rubber dingy in the middle of the Atlantic. When Jesus spoke about his spirit, he said that the Spirit would remind us of all he had said to us. Quite often, it is a question of forgetting, and we then cry out to God, as if he were at the other end of a 999 telephone line. God will be there, of course, at all times, but it is more advisable to avail of the help of a light-house, than to have to call on a life-boat. There is no need to wait for disaster to strike, because God is just as reliable in prevention as in curing. There is a rapid growth in preventative medicine in recent years, where more and more people are taking steps to preserve and maintain health, rather than wait until it is necessary to heal an illness. I often think that a doctor may very well know more about diseases than about health, because that would be the stress during the course of training. Christianity is very positive, and it gives reasons for doing something, rather than reasons for avoiding something else. Jesus speaks of coming to him to find rest, rather than avoiding something else that might upset us. There can be a level of pessimism in the world that can be soul-destroying. A man had climbed out on a bridge, and was threatening to jump in the river. A policeman was making his way along the bridge, and was trying his best to engage the man in conversation, to distract him. Eventually, he got quite close to him, and began talking to him. He tried to reason with him, and he even suggested a bargain. The policeman would listen for five minutes while the man told him what was wrong with life, and why he wanted to end it all, if the man was prepared also to listen for five minutes while the policeman told him what was good about life, and why it is worth living. The man agreed to this, and began a long list of things that made life impossible, and that made this world unbearable. The policeman had quite a job to stop him at the end of the five minutes. It was then the policeman's turn to speak for five minutes on the positive aspects of life and the world. He began with a few, and, after a while he ran out of something to say, so he reached out, took the man by the hand, and they both jumped in the river!

Failure, or fear of failure is often cause for anxiety, concern, and worry. I can lose control of my life, and give others power over me, so that I am always trying to be what they expect me to be. I can be a people-pleaser, with no boundaries of my own, and I simply cannot say 'No', so that I find myself agreeing to something that was not of my choice. I remember seeing an item on television one time, where a man was attempting to get into the *Guinness Book of Records* for spinning plates. He had a pile of plates, and very light rods, and the idea was to put a plate balancing on one of the rods, and to set it spinning, so that it would continue spinning for some time, before collapsing. The target was to get eighty-five plates spinning at the same time. It was nerve-racking even to watch him, because by the time he got to set up the fifth plate, the first one was losing momentum, and had begun to wobble. The audience got into the spirit of things, and they were screaming as plates wobbled dangerously, and the man got back to them just in time to give an extra flick. I remember taking a break from work a few years ago, and the feeling I had was of walking away from the plates, and letting them all crash down. I had a great sense of freedom. Regaining control of my life, and taking back the power I may have given others over me, is a very positive step towards healthy living. I've said it several times already, and I say it again, … in life, the miles stretch out ahead, but the things that trip me up are inside me. I may have such a poor self-image, that I crave affirmation and approval from others, and will do anything to get that approval.

Of all the apostles, Peter is my favourite. Peter seemed to always get it wrong, but there was never any doubt that he had a good heart. It is obvious Jesus was very fond of Peter, even if he had to call him to order on several occasions. On two special occasions, Peter showed what he thought of Jesus. When some of the disciples walked away, because they didn't like what Jesus was saying, he turned to Peter and the others, to ask 'Will you also go away?' To which Peter immediately replied 'Lord, to whom can we go? You alone have the words of eternal life.' On another occasion Jesus asked the apostles who they thought he was, and Peter immediately replied 'You are the Christ, the Son of the living God, who has come into the world.' Yes, Peter had the basics very right, indeed, and I'm absolutely sure that he was under no illusions about his own power and strength. In the Garden, he may well have been one of the first to run. Later that night, he was terrified of being exposed as one of Jesus' disciples, so he strongly denied that he knew Jesus. Later, Jesus looked at Peter, and poor Peter just melted. He went away, and cried his eyes out. He was not afraid or ashamed to admit that he had got it wrong. On the very same night, Judas let Jesus down as well, and got it very wrong. However, his biggest mistake was to think that this had put him outside of Jesus' love and acceptance. And so Judas went out and hanged himself, and there was nothing Jesus could do to stop him. No wonder Peter later wrote in one of his letters 'Always have a reason to give to those who ask you the reason for the hope that you have.' In other words, Peter considered that a Christian is someone who always has great hope, and when others notice this, and ask about it, it is important to be able to tell them why I have such hope.

I remember helping out one time in a Hospice situation, where I would call each evening to say Mass with a group of the patients. It was a Friday, and I was going down the country for the weekend. I noticed that Annie was getting very weak, and it was unlikely she would be here when I returned on Monday evening. I prayed with her, blessed her with oil, and spoke to her about dying. As I was leaving her, I held her hands and said 'Annie, God might call you over the weekend. Will you be afraid to meet him?' Instantly she answered, 'Father, I'm sure he's going to be awful glad to see me.' The saint is not the person who loves God, but the one who is convinced that God loves her. The more of my life I can hand over to God, the less burden I have to carry. I sometimes think of Jesus suggesting to me that we swop crosses! He tells me that I am sometimes burdened down with cares, worries, and decisions that he came to take from me, if I would only allow that. He knows they are too much for me, and that I cannot manage them on my own. On the other hand he wants to give

me his cross, which, he says, I must carry if I am to be one of
his disciples. His cross is not too well understood. Someone
gets a stroke, a baby is born with some physical or mental dis-
ability, or a person is crippled in an accident. To speak of such
things as crosses, is to greatly misunderstand the cross of
Christ. Such happenings are not crosses, because they happen to pagans and atheists as well. The cross is always a
good, is always a blessing, and such things are certainly not
blessings in themselves, even though, with God's help, they
can be turned into blessings. A cross is anything I have to do
as a direct result of my decision to walk in the Christian way,
to follow Jesus, to take him seriously. If I decide to walk in his
way, then I have to forgive, I have to share, I have to pray.
This cross is made up of the splinters of daily living, and
that's what Jesus means when he says that I must take up my
cross everyday, and follow him. It is a wise saying that the
person who has a 'Why' for doing something, will always
find a way to deal with the 'How'. We are followers of Jesus,
God-among-us, to whom nothing is impossible. At best my
life is often a choice between faith or insanity! I am strongly
suggesting faith, because life is just too changeable, and too
unpredictable for me to be able to manage it. It is a long long
way worse than trying to keeping eighty-five plates spinning
at the same time!

18 Hang in there

Imagine yourself standing against a wall, with both arms outstretched. You are on a cross, with one arm back trying to relive yesterday, called guilt, and the other trying to arrange to-morrow, called worry. This is where the Serenity Prayer comes in useful. The first part is 'Lord, give me the serenity to accept the things I cannot change.' There are two things in my life I cannot change. I cannot change yesterday. It went away at midnight, and will never return. The second thing I cannot change are the people in my life. I am powerless over persons, places, or things. The remainder of the prayer is 'Courage to change the things I can, and the wisdom to know the difference.' I cannot change yesterday, and I have no guarantee that I'll see to-morrow. George Burns, the American comic, died over a year ago, aged one hundred. Towards the end of his life he used joke that the first thing he did every morning, when he woke up, was to pick up the newspaper, look down the death columns, and if his name was not there, he got up! When I waken up each morning, I accept from God the gift of today. It is total gift, and it is significant that we call it the present. It is a gift that not everybody received, as is witnessed by the same death columns. The important thing about the gift it that written all over the box are the words 'batteries included'. With the day comes whatever I need to live today. Jesus calls this our daily bread, and it is included with the tickets, as it were. The secret of sanity is to keep life within the day, to live my life, one day at a time. I know a recovering alcoholic who, when he gets out of bed in the morning, goes on his knees, thanks God for the gift of today, and

then hands it back to him, asking him to take care of it for
him. He tells God that his life was in a mess when he was in
charge, and he doesn't want to do that again. Therefore, he
trusts God to run things for him today. At the end of the day,
before getting into bed, he goes on his knees again, to thank
God for taking good care of his day for him. It is important to
slow life down, to deal with it in twenty-four hour segments.
I sometimes think of my friend, who hands each day into
God's care; one of those days is going to be his last, and what
a wonderful way to prepare. He is not waiting till he dies to
hand his life over to God. As someone said 'Live each day as
if it was your last, and one day you will be right.'

I saw a poster somewhere, and the general drift of it went
something like this: 'I was regretting the past, and fearing the
future. Suddenly my Lord was speaking: "My name is I
AM".' He paused. I waited. He continued, 'When you live in
the past, with its mistakes, and regrets, it is hard. I am not
there. My name is not "I WAS". When you live in the future,
with its problems and fears, it is hard. I am not there. My
name is not "I WILL BE". When you live in this moment, it is
NOT hard. I am here. My name is "I AM".' God is totally a
God of NOW. If I can become a person of now, I will meet
God. I could well imagine that most people meet God for the
first time at the moment of death, when the running is finished, the worrying is ended, and the game is over. Sometimes
we hear the following expressions about people, 'He's all
over the place ... She's awfully scattered ... He badly needs
to get himself together.' The opposite to that is togetherness,
wholeness, wholesomeness, or holiness. It is about dropping
both arms, and meeting God today.

The telephone rang in this house, and it was answered in a
whisper by a tiny voice, that was obviously that of a child.
'Hello'. 'Is you father there?' 'No, I'm sorry he's busy.' 'Well,
can I speak to your mother?' 'No', came back the whisper,
'I'm sorry, she's busy.' 'Is there anyone else I can talk to? Is
there anyone else there?' 'There's the fire brigade, the ambu-

lance, and the police' was the whispered reply. 'Can I speak to one of the men from the fire brigade?' 'No, I'm sorry, they're busy'. 'Well, can I speak to the driver of the ambulance?' asked the man, with heightened voice, and impatient tone. 'No,' came the whispered reply, 'I'm sorry, he's busy.' 'Well, then', asked our friend, running out of patience, and getting more agitated, 'Can I speak to one of the policemen?' 'No', came the reply. 'I'm sorry, they're busy'. 'What's happening there?' roared our friend, 'What are they all doing there?' 'They're looking for me', came the whispered reply. I tell that story, because that's how it must look to Jesus looking on, as people are running in all directions, looking for something that is right there within their own hearts, should they choose to stop long enough to look.

I met a missioner home from Kenya some time ago, and I was really impressed as he spoke about the people among whom he had worked for the previous thirty years. It was obvious that he had a great love and respect for them. He admired their native wisdom, and their own special brand of theology. He was convinced they had a lot to teach us Europeans. This is one of many stories he told me. On the first Saturday of every month, he went into the bush with a jeep, and rounded up anybody needing to attend his clinic that day, when the flying doctors would pass through. Each month, there was a different kind of surgery offered, and this week it was harelips, and cleft palates. One young lad had a harelip, and, when the doctors were finished with him the priest was amazed at the excellent job they had done, leaving barely a sign of the harelip. He brought the young lad out of the clinic, and over to his father, who was seated under a tree. The boy bowed to the father, who placed a hand of blessing on his head, as was the custom, and that was it. The father didn't seem to notice the improvement in the boy's appearance. Then the women, including his mother, came along, and there was great excitement. They hugged him, examined his lip close up, brought him out from under the trees to have a good look at the transformation, and there was a great buzz of excitement in the air. Meanwhile the father was still sitting under the trees. This puzzled the missioner, so he went over to him, and asked him, 'Are you pleased with the job the doctors have done on your son?' 'Oh, yes', he replied. 'I am very pleased.' 'How come, then', asked the priest, 'you didn't show any signs of being greatly pleased when your son came out to you from the clinic?' 'I love my son', replied the father. 'If I showed any great signs of delight, it would have shown him that I did not really love him when he had a harelip. I still love him now the way I always did.' Once again, I use this story, because I believe it applies equally well to Jesus, who loves us just the way we are. He doesn't love me because I'm good. He loves me because he's good, and his love for me doesn't change. Guilt is not from God, and guilt can be very destructive. Jesus set a very high standard for how we are to love others. He asked us to love others as he loves us. Loving others includes loving myself, because if I do not have a healthy love for self, then God help my neighbour!

In recent years I spent some time living very near a harbour, and I was very conscious of the tide, as I looked out my window. At one time all the boats sat on the mud, as all the waters had left the harbour. Later, when I looked out, all the boats were afloat again. The rising tide had raised all the boats, the big ones as well as the small ones. Once again, I can apply this to the Lord. His Spirit within can bring everything within me to the surface, where it can be named, claimed, and tamed. The journey towards wholeness, wholesomeness, and hope is one of continually opening out. Life has often been compared to an onion, which has many layers, and can cause a few tears. I have a direct choice between revelation or cover-up. To the extent that I tend to cover things over, to that extent, I am unredeemed, because hiding is a direct inheritance of original sin. Openness to things the way they are is a clear sign that the Holy Spirit is at work. Acknowledging areas in need of salvation is freedom, not guilt. Christianity and guilt are incompatible. Guilt is not from God, and can be very negative and pessimistic. In the last book in the Bible, called the Book of Revelations, Satan is called the accuser of the brethren, because he accuses them day and night before God. It serves Satan's purpose that we should be burdened with guilt, and that such guilt might accumulate, to become such a heavy burden, that we lose hope, and despair. I believe that the only real sin a Christian can commit is to lose hope, and end up in despair. My reason for saying that, is because despair could prevent me bringing something to the Lord, something he would have no problem dealing with. If Judas had not gone off on his own, he might have had a chance to see love and acceptance in the eyes of Jesus, just as Peter had. To believe that anything I have done is outside of his love and forgiveness, is to fly in the face of everything Jesus has told us. Once again, Jesus lays great stress on us believing his promises, and trusting him to deliver on them.

There is a vast difference between being helpless, and being hopeless. The difference is so great, that I might say experiencing and accepting helplessness can be a virtue, while admitting to hopelessness can be a sin! The whole Christian message is about God coming to us, in our helplessness, and making it possible for us to live by his power, with a whole new hope, offering us a life beyond our wildest dreams. The paradox of this is that, the more conscious I am of my own powerlessness, the more powerful the Lord can work in me. Like St John the Baptist, the more I decrease, the more the Lord can increase. The more I get out of the way, the greater freedom the Lord has to work in me, and through me. I could easily fall into the trap of trying to have faith in my faith. I could easily over-emphasise my own contribution to all of this, and end up getting in the way of the Lord. My hope is based on Jesus, and on him only. It is based on his love and his promises, and not on anything I can do, or have done.

Life can be difficult, and there are times when it's not easy to retain hope and optimism. I am only human, and it is quite

normal to have my good days, and my bad days. The hope I
speak of, however, is part of the work of the Holy Spirit in my
soul, and is total gift, that rises above all my human weakness, and is in me, rather than of me. It is one of the fruits of
the Spirit, or the results of the Spirit living in me. If I see a tree
with apples on it, I will rightly conclude that it is an apple
tree. If I see the fruits of the Spirit in your life, I will rightly
conclude that you have the Spirit within you. 'You will receive power from on high', Jesus promised his apostles, 'and
you will be my witnesses to the ends of the earth.' In other
words, you will receive the power, but you must also accept
the responsibility that goes with such power. A very positive
witness is, in the words of St Peter, to always have a reason to
give those who ask you the reason for the hope that you have.
It is a long journey from the Fall until now, and throughout
that time, there is constant proof of the Lord's care and concern for his people. Even within the relatively short span of
my own life, I must be able to recognise many signs of his
care and concern for me. To think of what time may be left,
and to leave that to him, is not a great deal to ask for. I can
continue to worry, of course, but, as Jesus said, 'Will all this
worry add one minute to your life?' In fact, with the rise of
heart attacks, heart failures, and other coronary problems, it
is accepted that worrying and good health do not go together
at all. Worry could well be defined as not having enough faith
and trust in God. 'All will be well, and all manner of things
will be well' is a saying attributed to St Julian of Norwich.
What a wonderful Christian motto that would make! I could
do with a large poster at all points of my daily work, which
proclaims again and again 'All will be well, and all manner of
things will be well.'

I heard of something that happened to a friend of mine
one time. She began her day in a vile humour. She looked like
the weather forecast, when there is a low coming in over for
the day. Anyhow, whatever her husband said, he shouldn't
have said it, because he got a telling off. He knew it was

going to be one of those days, so he grabbed his lunch-box
and left for work earlier than usual. The children however,
were not so smart. One was doing his homework in the middle of the cornflakes, another couldn't find her socks, and a
third was looking for money for copies. The tension in the
kitchen was rising by the minute, and, eventually, all were
turfed out the door, without a parting hug. They brought a lot
of the tension with them, and, as they met their friends, they
ignored them, which caused further annoyance. Later, in
school, one was still so upset that, not only did he not know
the answer, he hadn't even heard the question! He got
thrown out of the class. By midday, the disquiet of this morning's kitchen had begun to spread around the parish!
Meanwhile, back in the kitchen, at eleven o' clock, the mother
was still in her dressing-gown, and ten cups of tea later, the
day wasn't getting any better! Then it hit her like a bolt of
lightening. 'My God', she said, 'nothing that happened in this
house this morning came from God.' This shocked her, because she is a good Christian woman. She reached for the bottle
of holy water, sprinkled it all over the place, and told Satan to
clear off, and leave her alone.(Satan is the only one you can
tell to go to hell!) Immediately, the cloud lifted, as it always
will, when we use the power and authority Jesus has given
us. She then phoned her husband, and told him it was OK to
come home! Jesus says 'I have given you full authority over
all the power of the evil one; nothing will harm you.' If she
had continued to forget that she had that authority, a week
later she would probably be on Valium, and a few weeks later
on the booze. I've seen a lot of people going down the tube,
because they either did not know they had this authority, or
they neglected to use it. Let me put it this way. Suppose you
are working for a man who bullies you, scolds you, humili-
ates you in front of the customers in his shop. He pays you a
mere pittance, and treats you like dirt. One day a gentleman
comes into the shop, and is shocked at what he sees and
hears, so he calls you aside, and offers you a job with him.

You accept the job, where you are completely in charge, where you have dignity, and respect, and you are well paid. Then one day, who enters that shop but your boss from your last job. Straightaway, he begins to order you around, to bully you, and to belittle you in front of the customers. What would you do? I hope you would get rid of him, and tell him that he no longer has any authority over you, and that you owe him nothing. You let him know who is boss around here! That is exactly our situation because of what Jesus has done for us. We are free, and we are nobody's slave, to be bullied and burdened, as if we had no rights. Jesus even went so far as to say that our names are registered as citizens of heaven. In other words, we are saved, we are on our way to heaven, and the onus is on us to look saved, and to look like people who know where we're going.

19 And then there's death

I did a video some years ago, called 'Death, a Fact of Life'. The opening shots were intended to grab attention. The first shot was a birth scene, where the baby was seen being born, and the cord was cut. The scene that immediately followed this was the straps being pulled up from the coffin, after it was lowered into the grave. The intention was to make a point. Life is a journey from one birth to another birth. I am born to die, and the very moment I am born I have taken my first step towards death. There is a journey from the womb life, to the womb of life, to the fullness of life. Once life begins, it never ends. If I drew a line along a wall, and off to the horizon, and then marked two X's on it, a few inches apart, it would help illustrate the fact that I spend a tiny part of my existence in the body. The body is not me. I am living in the body for a few short years. Then I will leave the body, and go on to the next stage of life. I have a donor card for the body, when I am finished with it, and anyone is welcome, who can find any parts that are still useful, after I have finished with them! What is left is called 'the remains', because that is what will remain after I have gone ahead to the third and final stage of life. The body is like the booster rockets on a space shuttle. They give propulsion, and direction, and are then discarded, when they fall back to earth. When I am launched, as it were, the body can then return to the clay from which it came. A man was strolling through a cemetery with his little four-year-old daughter. She pointed to the tomb stones, and asked him what they were for. He was really puzzled how best to explain something like this to a four-year-old. 'These were people who lived in those houses down there, and then, one day, God asked them to come and live with him in his house.' There was a moment's silence, and then another question. 'And, daddy, did they go off to live in holy God's house?' 'Yes', said the father, hoping to end the discussion. Then the little girl's eyes lit up, as she looked up at her dad and said, 'And guess what, daddy, I bet you when they went off to live in holy God's house, this is where they left their clothes.' And, you know something, she was spot-on. This is where they left their clothes, which they don't need now. I will never go into a coffin. The body I now live in will probably end up in a coffin, but, by then, I will have gone ahead, to become what I was created to be. It is after I pass through the second birth, which we call death, that I will become what God created me to be.

There were grubs crawling around in the bottom of a pond. They were talking, and wondering whatever happens to those among them who have crawled up the stems on top, and have never returned. They wondered what it might be like up there. They made an agreement with each other that the next grub to climb the stems of the lilies would return to tell the others what it was like up there. Sure enough, after some time, one felt drawn to the surface. He climbed to the top, and out on a leaf on the lily-pond. It was so bright here, so bright and so warm. It had been so dark and cold down below. Suddenly, something started to happen to him, as he began to change, to open out, to discover that he had two beautiful wings, that he had actually become a beautiful dragon-fly, which he was created to be, in the first place. He had no idea of this, as he thought he was supposed to remain a grub, or a caterpillar, all his life. He flew back and forth across the pond. He could see them below, but they could not see him. There was no way he could get back to them. After a while, he gave up trying, because, he concluded, 'Even if they could see me, they would never believe that a beautiful creature like me was ever one of them!' There is a very wide gap between one stage of life and the next. Imagine if an unborn baby could hear you clearly, as you speak to it. The frustration would be that not one word you could use would mean anything to the baby, with its little intelligence. Ireland, Dublin, water, light, … not one word you could use would mean a thing to the baby. We sometimes hear it said that no one comes back to tell us what it's like. I think it would be a waste of time, because it would be like the dragon-fly, and the grubs, or you and the unborn baby … the gap would be too wide, and, in the words of St Paul 'eye has not seen, nor ear heard, nor has it entered into the heart of people to imagine what God has in store for those who love him.'

Life itself can be very uncertain. Death is the only part of life that is sure and certain. What do we do about it? Face up to the reality now, and make that reality part of how I live my life, or keep it away out there in the future, and hope that God changes the way he does things by then?! Keep my head down, and don't even think about it, until it approaches me? One thing is certain: We shall all die one day. 'I shall die one day' can be too close for comfort, and so it's safer to keep it in the plural. An elderly husband and wife were chatting, and they made a pact. When one of them died, the other would mourn for only a limited time, then collect the insurance money, and have a really good holiday. After a while, the man said. 'Mary, do you know what I was thinking? When one of us dies, I think I'll probably go to New York!' Notice it's always the other people who die all the time. Some day … some day … it will be my turn, … 'the bell tolls for thee'. There was a rich man one time, who heard of a priest who was reputed to have a hot line to God. The man came to him with a most unusual request. He asked the priest if he could find out for him if he would definitely go to heaven when he died. The request was unusual, but the offer was tempting, because the man offered to make a very generous contribution to a new church being built. The priest agreed to take on the task. After a while, the man returned to ask him if he had received an answer to his query. The priest said he had. When the man asked what the answer was, the priest told him that he had good news for him, and he had bad news for him, and he asked which news the man wanted to hear first. The man was taken aback somewhat, but he asked for the good news first. The priest told him that, yes, he was going to heaven when he died. The man was delighted, and he felt that, with this good news, what could possibly be bad news after that. The priest replied 'The bad news is that you are going to-night!' It's strange, isn't it, that the second part should be seen as bad news? Everybody wants to go to heaven, but nobody wants to die!

Life in the womb is preparing the baby for life on this earth, just as life here now is in preparation for the third, and final stage of life. In some ways, it could be said that death is the greatest kick of all, and that's why it's kept until last. For the mother, that first birth is sometimes followed by post-natal depression, just as the second birth is followed by bereave-ment. There is an exact parallel between both events. A worthwhile life was described thus by someone: When you were born, you alone cried, while everyone else was very happy. Live your life in such a way that, when you die, you will be happy, and everyone else will be crying. Or, as Mark Twain put it, 'Live your life in such a way that when you die, even the undertaker will be sorry!' Life is a constant struggle, a con-tinual tension between what I want and what I need, between what I want to do, and what I ought to do. If you ever waken up some morning, and your life is the way you had always wanted it, the way it ought to be, don't move, ... just stay where you are, and wait till the undertaker arrives!

A cow and a pig were out for a walk one day. The pig was very depressed, and the cow asked the reason why this was so. The pig complained that nobody liked him. Whenever they spoke about him, their language was quite offensive. Someone was said to eat like a pig, another was said to snore like a pig, while a mother told her son that his bedroom was like a pig-sty. 'They never use language like that, when they speak about you', said the pig. 'When they speak about you, they use very respectful language. For example, they speak about a milking parlour. It's all so proper and correct.' 'But there's a good reason for that', replied the cow. 'look at all I give them. I give them milk, butter, cheese, and cream.' 'But what about me?' asked the pig. 'I give them bacon, ham, and pork.' 'That's right', replied the cow, 'but there's a vast difference in the giving.' 'How is that?' asked the pig. 'I give it to them while I'm still alive', said the cow. 'They have to kill you to get anything from you.' God gives me nothing for myself, not even the gift of life. Anything I keep to myself during life, when I die, it dies too.

If the unborn baby could think, it would be terrified of dying, because it is moving out of the only world it knows. Once there were twin boys in their mother's womb. After some time, they became aware of the cord, and, after further discussion and examination, they decided that their mother must really love them, because she was sharing her very life with them. Some time further on, they became aware of changes occurring in themselves. They noticed tiny nails appearing on their fingers; they noticed little eye-brows, eye-lashes, etc. They wondered what this could mean. Then one of them suggested that they may be getting ready to be born. The other little guy cringed, and said 'I don't want to be born. I want to stay where I am.' 'But we have to be born', said the other little guy. 'We cannot stay here all our lives.' 'How do you know there's any life after this? Have you ever seen any one that was born? Did any of them ever come back to tell us what it's like?' 'There just has to be life after this. If this is it, it makes no sense at all. I honestly believe that we are here preparing for the next stage, whatever that will be.' 'But how do you know there's a mother? What does she look like? Have you ever seen her? I bet you we only invented her for our own security.' And so, the argument went back and forth. One was already a little atheist, while the other was a man of faith, which, in simple English, meant that he believed something, but had proof for nothing! And finally the time came, and they were born. When it was safe to do so, they opened their eyes, and found themselves looking up into the face of their mother. They looked at each other, as if to say 'Weren't we very foolish. There was no way we could ever have imagined what this was going to be like. It is now obvious that we had to be born to get an idea.' And so it is with us, now. We can argue and argue till the cows come home, but we will really have to pass through the next birth before we'll have any idea what it's all about.

Another way of looking at it, is to imagine seeds sown in the ground. They lie there, unaware of what is happening above the ground. They actually have to give what life they have, and then they die, but they could never imagine the whole new life that has emerged above the ground. How could the acorn recognise itself in the oak tree, or the tiny mustard seed understand that the large tree could ever come from something as tiny as it? For new life in spring, there has to be death, and as we admire the daffodils, and all the other beautiful spring flowers, we can easily forget that there are empty, lifeless shells, shrivelling away under the earth, and it is from those deaths that this new life has come.

When someone dies, they don't go away, they simply go ahead to the next stage, and we are certain to catch up with them. Death is like the horizon out there. The horizon is the limit of my vision, even though I know there is so much more out there than that. Parents are in the park with their children. Some of the kids run ahead, over the brow of the hill, where they hide, waiting on the parents to catch up with them. There has been a lot written in recent years about the near-death experience. It is called near-death, because it is the experience of someone who was clinically dead, but, thanks to electric shock, or some special machine, the heart was set going again, and, so they continued to live. Many of these people speak of that experience in very clear and definite terms. The one thing that all such accounts seem to have in common is the fact that family members who had gone ahead were seen to approach, as if to welcome … and then the person was revived. The common feeling they all seem to share is a great feeling of disappointment, because they had begun to experience an extraordinary level of peace, and the joy up ahead seemed very real, indeed. They felt cheated to have been revived, and all of them say that any fear they had of dying is totally gone.

One of the great experiences of death must be to get out of the body. We know no other kind of existence, and so we cannot possibly appreciate just how restricting the body really is. We are so limited in our ability to see, hear, understand, or act. We are subject to so many pressures, emotions, and simple pains and aches. St Paul called the body a prison, and he longed to be free. Imagine having an over-view of everything, where I can see myself in relationship to everybody and everything on this planet. People today try to alert us to some of that, when they speak about our responsibility for the environment. To see myself within the context of the greater plan of creation. I used this image in a previous chapter, but I'll refer to it again. There is a scene of rare beauty, a picture that stretches the length of a wall here beside me. A cloth covers it, and but for a hole of about one inch square, I cannot see the picture. The tiny part I can see, a few trees, and some grass, is my contribution to the whole. At the moment of death, the cloth is swept away, and I will have my eyes and mouth wide open in amazement for all eternity at the beauty, and the sheer joy of knowing that I was, and am part of this. Another image I have used already is the idea that I am standing in a tall cardboard box, with sides so high that I cannot glimpse over them. At the moment of death, the sides of the box fall away, and I look around with gasps of wonder at a beauty that was there all the time, but I was unable to see it. At the moment of death, the eyes of the body close, and the eyes of the soul open, and, for the first time ever, I really can see. 'I can see clearly now' is a fitting chorus for people at that moment of death.

20 Happy ever after

Remember the raisins in the dough that we spoke about in the first chapter? Well there is one raisin, or human weakness, that we all share: we shall all one day die. As I said back then, Jesus took on our human weaknesses, one after another. Now, the final weakness was death, and so, Jesus had to face up to this one, as well. It was absolutely essential that he prove to us, beyond all doubt, that we are free. We say 'Lord, by your cross and resurrection, you have set us free.' And again, 'Dying you destroyed our death, rising you restored our life.' There were several times when the Jewish leaders tried to arrest Jesus, but, each time he just walked freely away, or disappeared from their midst. In the Garden of Gethsemane, he asked the mob 'Who are you looking for?', they replied 'Jesus of Nazareth', and, as he said 'I am he', they all fell backwards. In other words, Jesus was showing that he was serious when he had said 'No one takes my life from me. I freely lay down my life, and I will take it up again.' In other words, they arrested Jesus, and killed him, when he decided that 'the time had come', as he told his apostles. On many occasions, Jesus told his disciples that he would die, but that he would return. He never once mentioned his death, without referring to the fact that he would rise again. Therefore, after his resurrection on Easter morning, he spent the next forty days with his apostles, continually proving to them that he was alive and well, and was certainly not a ghost. He asked for food to eat, he invited Thomas to touch him, he prepared a meal for them on the seashore. Later on, they were to be his witnesses to the ends of the earth, and a top priority in that witnessing would be the fact that he had passed through death, and returned to clearly prove that there was life beyond the grave. In fact, I sometimes think that the problem Jesus could have with us, is that there is not enough life this side of the grave. Again and again, Jesus appeared to his apostles, leaving them in no doubt that he was, indeed, alive. He walked along the road towards Emmaus with two of them, who failed to recognise him. There is a certain humourous dimension to this, because he asked them why they were so down-cast, and they were amazed that he hadn't heard what had happened to Jesus, who had been killed a few days previously. They said what made the disappointment worse was that they had thought he was really going to turn out to be somebody worthwhile, who would set them free from their enemies. Once again, the idea of political freedom was the only idea that seems to have stuck with his disciples. Jesus brought them back through the Scriptures, and showed that all of this was foretold by the prophets, and it all had happened as was told. By the time they realised who he was, he disappeared from their sight.

On the morning of the resurrection, Mary Magdalene was crying at the side of the tomb, when Jesus appeared to her. He told her to tell his disciples that he had risen, as he promised, and that he would meet them in Galilee. Imagine the excitement, as Mary, and her friends rushed off to tell the others the good news they had just received. Jesus had overcome the final enemy, death, and he was alive. The words 'He is alive' became a clarion call for the disciples, and this would later be central to the message they would have to bring to others. I sometimes think of the predicament of a preacher or teacher, who is travelling towards Emmaus, rather than to Galilee. The guys on their way to Emmaus had heard a rumour that Jesus was alive, while Mary Magdalene had actually met him! When the apostles were arrested, after Pentecost, they were accused of spreading a rumour that the man the leaders had killed was alive. This was considered very upsetting news to those who thought they had got rid of that man Jesus, who opposed them, and their way of life. What was good news for one group was bad news for the others.

Water represented death for the Hebrews. They had to pass through the waters of the Red Sea, before entering the Promised Land. Jesus walked on water, to prove to the apostles that he had control over death. Peter asked if he might be free from the fear of death, so Jesus invited him to come towards him, walking on the waters. Peter stepped over the side of the boat, and was actually walking on the water, when he took his eyes off Jesus, and became very conscious of the wind and the waves. He lost his nerve, and began to sink. Jesus reached out a hand, and took hold of Peter, saying 'Oh why did you doubt, you of little faith.' Later, St Paul would say that we must keep our eyes fixed on Jesus. He is our Moses, leading us through the desert of life, into the Promised Land. If I am to follow a leader, I must always keep my eye on him. Jesus compared himself to a shepherd. One of my clearest memories of visiting the Holy Land, is that of the shepherds and their sheep. In the sweltering heat, it always impressed me to see a shepherd standing alone among his sheep, as they searched for grass among the sands. At night-time, the sheep were led into a cave on the hillside, and the shepherd slept at the entrance. In other words, if the sheep were attacked it would literally be over the dead body of the shepherd. On other occasions, I saw a shepherd, with a long line of sheep, in single file, walking behind him. Wherever he went, the sheep followed. It is also a known fact that, in the midst of one of the many sudden thunder storms that happen there on a regular basis, the sheep never look up at the sky; rather do they look towards the shepherd, and move closer to him. His listeners would have understood exactly what Jesus meant, because he used examples from their everyday experiences. On Easter morning, the Good Shepherd was bringing his sheep safely through the portals of death. For the Christian, death was no longer to hold any fear. The final enemy had been overcome, and we were free. John the Baptist's father, Zachary, said that when the Messiah would gain the victory, we would be free from fear, and safe from the hands of our foes, so that we could serve the Lord in holiness all the days of our lives, in his presence.

Death, for the Christian, is not just something that happens at the end of life. Life can be a whole series of dyings, every time I put someone before myself, and every time I die to my selfishness, for the sake of another. The cross of Calvary was intended for Barabbas, but Jesus took his place, and Barabbas went free. Barabbas represents all of us. Jesus put us in front of himself. Even while on the cross, he was dying in more ways than physically. He asked the Father to forgive those who were killing him, he asked John to take care of his mother, and he entrusted John to her care. He promised heaven to one of the men on another cross beside him. When he had done all that dying, the physical dying was easy. Death is like a pile of sand at the end of my life, that I can take and sprinkle, a little every day during life, so that, when I get to the end, there'll be no more dying to do. On the other hand, if I wait till the end of my life to die, it will be too late. A poor beggarman heard that someone called the King of Kings was coming to a certain village. The beggarman wasn't sure what this title could mean, but it obviously implied that he was a very wealthy man. This was an opportunity to do some worthwhile begging, so off he set to meet this wealthy person. There was quite a crowd when he arrived in the village, so he had to wait for many hours before he got a chance to be ushered into the presence of this very important person. When his turn came, his mind was racing with all he was going to ask for. Before he got a word out of his mouth, the King of Kings said 'Well, my good man, and what do you have for me?' 'Me? Me?' asked the beggarman. 'I don't have anything for you.' 'But you must' replied the king. 'Everybody has something to give.' The beggarman insisted that he had nothing to give, while the king was equally insistent that he must have something. Finally, with great annoyance, and in frustration, the beggarman took a piece of cloth from his pocket, in which he kept some grain, for chewing as he walked around. He opened the cloth, took two grains of wheat, and gave them to the King of Kings, who then turned and walked away. The beggarman was furious. He stomped out of the building, and strode off down the road, feeling that he had been made look like a complete fool. When he had walked about a mile, he took out the cloth, to get some grains to chew, and was totally amazed to see, among the grains of wheat, two grains of gold. He thumped his forehead in disgust, as he muttered 'You fool! Why didn't you give them all away?' That's what it could feel like at the end of my life, when I realise how much of life I had lived for myself. Only those parts of life which were given away in the service of others have an eternal value.

There is a very true saying that as you live, so shall you die. Life now is but a preparation for what is to follow. We are a pilgrim people, always on our way, never staying more than sixty seconds in any one minute. Life is constantly in a state of flux, and change, and experience is a very good school, even if the fees are often very high. Jesus is travelling the road with us, and if we listen to him, he will guide us along his way. He says that no one comes to the Father except through him. Everybody that ever lived will come face to face with Jesus, at least once, and will have to decide for him, or against him. About two-thirds of the people in the world die without having heard about Jesus, but, even they, at that moment of death, will be faced with the option, and will be asked to made a decision. They will not arrive there totally unprepared, of course, because even the most primitive caveman knew there was a God, even though he thought that it was the sun, the wind, or the sky. Everybody that ever lived has had some feeling about a life after death, even if they called it the spirit world, the happy hunting ground, or crossing the Jordan. And everybody has a conscience, just as a dog can look guilty when he does something wrong. Everybody who died before Jesus, were all dressed up, with nowhere to go, as it were, because admission into heaven was not possible until Jesus had returned in triumph. From that moment on, each person is brought face to face with Jesus, and asked to decide. Nobody, but nobody comes to the Father but through Jesus. He said that he was the gate to the sheep-fold, and there is only one way to enter. There was an accident down the road, and a young lad was killed. Was he ready to meet God? No matter what good or evil he did in life, like the good thief on Calvary, he will be given one last chance to say 'yes'. God is a God of infinite justice, and everybody comes before him with an equal chance of entry into the fullness of his kingdom. For us Christians, our lives are expected to be a whole series of 'yeses', and this is thought of as the best possible preparation for that final 'yes'.

The king was all powerful, and the fool was a fool. One day, the king gave the fool a rod, and told him to hold on to it, and he was to give it away if he ever came across a bigger fool than himself. Many years went by. The king grew old, and was on his death-bed. He sent for his courtiers, his body-guard, and the fool, and he told them that he was about to set off on a long long journey, from which he did not expect to return. The fool spoke up 'Majesty, on other occasions, before you set out on a journey, you always sent servants and courtiers ahead, to prepare for your journey, and your arrival at wherever you were going. Might I ask you what preparations you have made for this particularly long journey?' 'Alas,' said the king, 'I have made no preparations for this journey. I am not at all prepared for it.' 'Then', said the fool, 'take this rod, because, at last, I have found a fool greater than myself.' God is not one who is into 'I told you so', but, if he were, he might surely have many opportunities to say this. I often wonder if hiding, hedging, avoiding, and making excuses is a direct result of original sin, because all diets start on Monday, and we are certainly going to take this dying bit very seriously ... some other time. There is nothing more powerful than an idea whose time has come.

Thérèse of Lisieux and Padre Pio said that their real work would begin after they died, and I honestly believe that to be so. Jesus' work, or Mary's work, did not cease when they died. They still continue to look out for us, and to look after us. I had the privilege, some years ago, of celebrating Mass every day with a small group in a Hospice for the dying. I had a continual opportunity to bring many of them to the gates of death, over a two or three-year period. I spoke to most of them about what Thérèse and Padre Pio had said, and I gave them special 'missions' to take care of, some person or family in a mess, some situation that looked hopeless. I do not, for a moment, think it could be a coincidence, but I always watched, with amazement, to see something good happen in what had been a hopeless situation. One elderly lady was dying, and she knew a young woman whose life was badly messed up. I asked her to 'adopt' this young woman when she arrived safely home in the next life, as the thief on the cross asked Jesus to remember him when he came into his kingdom. Anyhow, naturally, the young woman knew nothing at all about what I had spoken of, nor does she know, to this day. About three weeks after the old lady died, I received a letter from the woman giving me the details of a remarkable dream she had, which had stirred up a whole conversion experience in her soul. The old lady came to her in the dream, and the encounter, and what was said, was so real that, when the young woman woke up, she acted on the advice given, and her life has since turned dramatically around. I have seen this happen on many occasions, to the point where I came to expect it to happen. I remember promising one young woman that I would do her funeral, but that it would be up to her to 'fix it', because the funeral was going to be in Mayo, and I wasn't even sure I would be in the country at the time. Anyhow, I was in Tralee, beginning a six-day Retreat, when I knew that I should be in Mayo for a funeral that evening and the following morning. I'm glad I do not have the gift of bi-location, of being in two places at the same time, because I often have more than enough problems in any one place, without doubling my trouble. Anyone, just as I wondered how she was going to 'fix' this one, one of the people on Retreat came to tell me that she had a set of videos I had made some time before that, that she had brought them along, and she wondered if the group might have a chance to watch them over the next week. The videos included six talks, before a group in a studio, and the talks covered the basic message of the gospel. I showed her where the video machine was, put her in charge, and went off to Mayo to do the funeral. While I was there, I was also giving six talks to a very enthusiastic group back in Tralee! I could continue with such incidents in a separate book, but I give these few as examples of something that I know to be true.

Grief is the price we pay for love, and if I have any capacity for love, I should always keep a few tissues around. If you never want to cry at a funeral, don't ever love anyone, … and that would be a terrible price to pay to avoid a few tears. Jesus cried at the tomb of Lazarus. They were tears of love, and not of despair. I think it is lovely, and very natural that, even though I believe my mother is happy with God, I can cry at her funeral, because I miss her, and life, without her, will never be the same. Funerals are geared more towards the bereaved than the deceased. The readings, homily, etc, are directed to those present, rather than to the deceased. Bereavement is a process, and there is no safe short-cut through it. It is like the amputation of a leg. I will walk again, but it would be foolish to hurry up the process. The very pain is healing, and taking something to numb the pain is only delaying facing up to reality. If I don't cry now, I will scream later.

I remember being in Cobh some years ago when the QE2 visited there. Everybody, but everybody was there. Bands playing, small aircraft hovering overhead, boats of all de-

scriptions escorting her into the harbour. She left very early
the following morning, and I had a bird's-eye view from my
bedroom window as that majestic giant sailed off towards the
horizon. I actually thought of the concept of death, as I saw
her disappear over the horizon, knowing that she was still as
majestic as ever, and probably, as I was saying 'There she
goes', someone in Wales was saying 'Here she comes.' If I
may continue with the idea of an ocean liner, by way of finishing this chapter. When a passenger boat comes within
sight of Cobh, Southampton, or New York, she is stopped.
Then a pilot comes out from the harbour in a tug-boat, climbs
on board, and brings her into harbour. Jesus is our pilot, who
is willing to come out to meet us at any distance, and to bring
us safely home. Home where we will meet all our old friends,
and never have to say good-bye again.

The young mother set her feet on the road of life. 'Is the
way long?' she asked. 'Yes', said the guide 'and the way is
rough, and you will be old before you reach the end of it.' But
the young mother was happy, as she played with her children, and gathered flowers with them along the way. 'Surely'
she said 'nothing could ever be better than these years.' And
they moved on, and there was a hill ahead, and the children
grew tired, and the mother was tired, but all the time she kept
saying 'A little further, and we're there'. And they struggled
and reached the top, and the children said 'Mother, we never
could have made it without you.' And the mother, when she
lay down that night, said 'This is a brighter and better day
than yesterday, because today I showed my children
courage'. And the next day there were clouds, clouds of war,
hatred, and evil. And the mother said 'Lift your eyes. Lift
your eyes towards the stars.' And they clung to her, to her
faith, and to her hope, and they were safe and saved, and that
night, when she lay down to sleep, the mother said 'This is
brighter than the brightest day, because today, I have shown
my children God.' And the weeks passed, and the months,
and the years. And the mother grew old, and was little and

stooped. But her children were strong, and tall, and walked with confidence. When she was tired they carried her, because she was a burden to no one. Finally they came to a gate, with golden gates flung wide. And the mother said 'I have reached the end of my journey. Now I know that the end is so much more beautiful than the beginning, because my children can walk with courage, and their children after them.' And her children said 'Mother, you will always walk with us, even when you have gone through those gates.' And they stood and watched her, as she walked on alone, and the gates closed behind her. And her children said 'A mother like ours is more than a memory. She is a living presence.'